John Beecher

COLLECTED POEMS
1924–1974

COLLECTED POEMS
1924–1974

John Beecher

MACMILLAN PUBLISHING CO., INC.
New York

COLLIER MACMILLAN PUBLISHERS
London

Library of Congress Cataloging in Publication Data

Beecher, John, 1904–
Collected poems, 1924–1974.

I. Title.
PS3503.E233A6   1974   811'.5'4   73–10560
ISBN 0–02–508310–4

Macmillan Publishing Co., Inc.
866 Third Avenue, New York, N.Y. 10022
Collier-Macmillan Canada Ltd.

Second Printing 1975

Printed in the United States of America

Once more for Barbara

CONTENTS

IV. POEMS, 1941–1944

V. OBSERVE THE TIME,
An Everyday Tragedy in Verse, 1955

VI. POEMS, 1955–1960

VII.   PHANTOM CITY, *A Ghost Town Gallery, 1961*

VIII.   POEMS, 1961–1974

Acknowledgments

Many of the poems in this book have appeared in journals to which acknowledgments were made in my previous collections, *Report to the Stockholders and Other Poems* (1962), *To Live and Die in Dixie* (1966), and *Hear the Wind Blow!* (1968). A number of the poems collected here for the first time received prior publication in *The Bookman, Foxfire, Latitudes, The New Mexico Review, North Shore, PM, Twice A Year*, and *The South Florida Review*. An even larger number of the uncollected poems are making their original appearance in these pages.

The 136 poems that follow comprise just about all my published verse to date. I have excluded a body of highly personal poetry because it belongs more properly to the autobiography on which I am presently working. I have also excluded what seemed apprentice work, with one exception, "Big Boy," the first poem I ever wrote. Originally published in *The Bookman*, a well-regarded literary magazine of the twenties, "Big Boy" was reprinted in *The Literary Digest* as an example of antipoetic and verbally shocking trends. Thereupon it was defiantly set to music and publicly sung by the Apollo Male Chorus of Pittsburgh. It was climactically anthologized in a college poetry textbook, *Modern Verse*, edited by Anita Forbes and published by Henry Holt and Company. Although I denied it entrance to previous collections, I was unable to resist including the poem in the present volume. Perhaps it may serve as a benchmark from which to measure my progress since I was a very angry young man of twenty in a Birmingham steel mill half a century ago.

Those who may wish to examine the poems I omitted from this collection, as well as the many versions through which the poems included herein have passed, may find all these materials in the microfilmed edition of my complete works and personal papers issued by the Microfilming Corporation of America.

J. B.

Poetry for Survival

Hitler was *kaput* and the German High Command had surrendered. The stink of unexcavated corpses still hung over the rubble of the cities bombed out by our planes. General Eisenhower had issued an order prohibiting fraternization with the German population, so I fraternized with DPs instead, freed POWs, ex-slave laborers. My best friend was a Russian. It was not yet forbidden to fraternize with Russians. This came later.

My Russian friend and I had both been seafaring men in the war. He was a lieutenant commander in the Soviet Navy. Despite this he was a highly cultivated man. He loved poetry, for example. He took to me specially because I had published a couple of volumes of poetry before the war. He spoke very good English. He told me he had been captured when the Nazi invaders overran the great naval base guarding Leningrad in 1941. For four years he had been a prisoner of the Gestapo, who had used him as an interpreter in their interrogation chambers where even the ceilings, he said, were blood-splashed. His German and French were as good as his English. The Gestapo had allowed him to retain in his cell a single book, the poems of Alexander Pushkin. My friend told me that this book literally kept him alive through four years of unmitigated horror and degradation. When we parted to return to our respective homelands, he gave me his Pushkin for a remembrance.

Although my Russian friend had promised to write, I never heard from him. Stalin usually dispatched returned prisoners of the Germans directly to Arctic labor camps where Pushkin was not allowed past the gate. So my friend probably perished. I fared somewhat better in free America. During the McCarthy era I was fired from my job as a professor of sociology and blacklisted for refusing to sign a "loyalty" oath subsequently found unconstitutional by the Supreme Court. This took seventeen years. But I was lucky. I got off the blacklist in only nine years. During that period of what has been called "internal exile" I reconverted myself from a sociologist into a poet again. Of course nobody dared to print what I wrote. So I taught myself to print and became my own publisher. My Russian friend was right. Poetry can save your life.

John Beecher
Worcester Poetry Festival
1971

I

POEMS
1924–1940

REPORT TO THE STOCKHOLDERS

I

he fell off his crane
and his head hit the steel floor and broke like an egg
he lived a couple of hours with his brains bubbling out
and then he died
and the safety clerk made out a report saying
it was carelessness
and the craneman should have known better
from twenty years experience
than not to watch his step
and slip in some grease on top of his crane
and then the safety clerk told the superintendent
he'd ought to fix that guardrail

II

out at the open hearth
they all went to see the picture
called **Men of Steel**
about a third-helper who
worked up to the top
and married the president's daughter
and they liked the picture
because it was different

III

a ladle burned through
and he got a shoeful of steel
so they took up a collection through the mill
and some gave two bits
and some gave four
because there's no telling when

IV

the stopper-maker
puts a sleeve brick on an iron rod
and then a dab of mortar
and then another sleeve brick

and another dab of mortar
and when he has put fourteen sleeve bricks on
and fourteen dabs of mortar
and fitted on the head
he picks up another rod
and makes another stopper

V

a hot metal car ran over the Negro switchman's leg
and nobody expected to see him around here again
except maybe on the street with a tin cup
but the superintendent saw what an ad
the Negro would make with his peg leg
so he hung a sandwich on him
with safety slogans
and he told the Negro just to keep walking
all day up and down the plant
and be an example

VI

he didn't understand why he was laid off
when he'd been doing his work
on the pouring tables OK
and when men with less age than he had
weren't laid off
and he wanted to know why
but the superintendent told him to get the hell out
so he swung on the superintendent's jaw
and the cops came and took him away

VII

he's been working around here ever since there was
    a plant
he started off carrying tests when he was fourteen
and then he third-helped
and then he second-helped
and then he first-helped
and when he got to be sixty years old
and was almost blind from looking into furnaces
the bosses let him
carry tests again

VIII

he shouldn't have loaded and wheeled
a thousand pounds of manganese
before the cut in his belly was healed
but he had to pay his hospital bill
and he had to eat
he thought he had to eat
but he found out
he was wrong

IX

in the company quarters
you've got a steelplant in your backyard
very convenient
gongs bells whistles mudguns steamhammers and slag-
    pots blowing up
you get so you sleep through it
but when the plant shuts down
you can't sleep for the quiet

A MILLION DAYS, A MILLION DOLLARS
Eight Original Work Songs

The Check Board

Las night hangs ma check on de big check boa'd
Mawnin sees it hangin jessa same
Nigger git yo number an lif up yo load
Got a steel mill number, ain' got no name

Ore Train

Stan back, stan back
fum dat red flappin flag at de track
see de big jack
slickery an black

sparkin up de stack
stompin upgrade wid fo'ty cars of o'

Wheelbarrow Song

De sun's a big wheel rollin aroun
done rolled clean away fum dis heah town
rollin now under de groun
roll aroun sun
an den my wheelin's done

Day Turn and Night Turn

Buddy keep yo wuk close on
till de big jim whistle's done blown

Buddy lemme off an I's long gone
sof bed say she wan me ona phone

Sunday's Done Gone

Sunday's done gone
daytime's gone
dark dark dark
iron bells is ringin
churchtime's come
church time's come
praise the Lord for Sunday
praise praise praise
Monday's tomorrow
worktime's tomorrow
work folks work
Monday's tomorrow
Sunday's done gone
praise the Lord for Sunday
Monday's tomorrow

Watch Yo Step

Henry Mathews was a blas furnace man
He slung a sledge an he shovel san
Watch yo step, o watch yo step
Henry stepped in where de hot iron ran

Dey sawed off his leg
An give him a peg
An Henry went to wuk on de slag pot car
Watch yo step, o watch yo step
Henry fell in when dey dumped dat car

Dey dug up de slag an dey hunted right smart
Watch yo step, o watch yo step
All what dey foun was his bleedin heart

Convict Mine Reveille

Wake up mens an git yo fo o'clock cawfeh
day's done come to dig yo task
night's done gone but day woan las
wake up mens an pick dat coal
les hear dem hobnails hit dat flo
wake up
wake up
wake up mens an git yo fo o'clock cawfeh

It Won't Be Long

a stockhouse loader hammers on a gong
hammers out a song
on a gong
"it woan be long it woan be long"
two o'clock at night in the blast furnace casthouse
big wheels churning in the steamdamp blasthouse
faces flaring in the glow of coke
the red moon glaring through a mask of smoke
"it woan be long"

13 HOUR NIGHT SHIFT

You feel the day coming
inside you first
You go weak

You could go to sleep anywhere
like the test-boy in the aluminum box
wedged in with his knees drawn up and his head between them
sleeping
and the slag-hole gang
stretched out under the pouring tables on the dirt
and in the tunnels beneath the furnaces
like dead drunks
or a battlefield
When you stand still you drop off
and even when you keep moving
you must sleep a little with your eyes open
because your thoughts are full of short blanks
like the current going off a second and then coming on

BIG BOY

Skirt turned you down
Because you worked in a steel mill?
Told it over town,
Gave you the gate, laughed fit to kill?
Hell, what do you expect?
You can't help that, big boy!

Burns on your eye,
On your arms, your chest, your hands?
Goin' to cry?
Them things an open hearth feller stands.
Damn, snap to, you, buck up.
Make the best of it, big boy!

Can't stand the work?
Back sore, shovel handle cuts like a knife?
How can you shirk?
You got to eat, ain't you, in this dirty life?
Hell, swing on to that hammer.
Put your back into it, big boy!

Hop on a freight?
Go some place where a man's got a chance?
That ain't your fate!
Weak head, strong back, and you got on pants.
Why, you're as dumb as me!
What else can you do, big boy?

Wish you could die,
Wish 'twas pneumonia 'stead of smoke has got you to coughin'?
Wish you could lie
Under the ground in a varnished pine coffin?
Christ, you wish you was dead?
Huh, you ain't got nothin' on me, big boy!

Ensley Steel Works, 1924

WHITE-EYE

he couldn't remember ever such a hot night as this was
with the wind off the furnaces
what wind there was
he could have drunk the waterworks dry
only he dasen't
fear of cramps
he said what a hot night it was
and they said he must be getting too old for the work
yes he was old
fifty years old
he felt of his arms and legs
not as hard as once but hard
it wasn't them but something else wore out

he tapped number 9
then shoveled a good round of bottom
usually he sweat good but tonight he didn't
he felt like he was going to white-eye

so he asked off from the melter
and went to his locker to change clothes
in a tunnel under the furnaces
it was hotter down here than on top
he'd got to get out of here quick
he pulled off his shirt
and kicked off his pants
and leaned over to unlace his shoes
but didn't get up
because a cramp like a bonfire of his guts
downed him and dug his nose in the dirt
and he would have died if a Negro hadn't come that way
lucky for him
and dragged him to a shower
and held him under the hot water
till the cramp let go

he put in two weeks in bed
and when the money was nearly played out
he came back to work hoping nobody had his job
and wondering
how long before somebody would

BRICKROLLER

it was still a week to payday and he needed money bad
he had commissary checks enough to eat on
but he needed cash
he had to have a dollar
he stood behind the railing
gripping it hard
and looked at the bossmen in the office
until one of them noticed him and yelled
what you want nigger?
please whitefolks gimme a cash advance for a dollar

Jesus Christ get to hell outa here
what you think this is?
if you needed money you'd ask for five dollars
we ain't giving advances for a dollar
so he stopped in a loan shark's when he got off work
and swapped his commissary checks
for a dollar in cash

OLD MAN JOHN THE MELTER

old man John the melter
wouldn't tap steel till it was right
and he let the superintendents rave
he didn't give a damn about tonnage
but he did give a damn about steel
so they put him on the street
but he had plenty of money
and he drove up and down in his "Wily Knecht"
a floatin pallus he called it
with a Pittsburg stogie in his whiskers
and played poker at the Elks club
and the steel got sorrier and sorrier
and rails got to breaking under trains
and the railroads quit buying
and the mill shut down
and then the superintendents asked old man John
to come and tell them what was wrong with the steel
and he told them
too many superintendents

RUN OF THE MINE

I

I went into tight places for them (he said)
when the inspector had condemned a gallery
I went in and I got men to go with me
and we dug coal and kept our mouths shut
and I thought when the time came I needed it
they would go into a tight place for me
but because I had a foaming fit on the job
from high blood pressure and because I was old
and they thought I might cost them money
if I died at work in the mine
they fired me and put *unsatisfactory*
on my discharge slip and when I wanted to know
what unsatisfactory thing I had done
they said to come back next week for a statement

II

he went to work in Pennsylvania
up north where he could earn more mining
and every month for three years he sent money home
to keep up the payments on the house and furniture
and when he couldn't stay away from his wife
and children in the south any longer
he came home to his old job at Camp Seven
that year it rained and rained and then rained
and though his house like all the other houses there
was perched on stilts to escape the regular floods
the water came in and kept on rising
and when it went down the cheap veneer
of the just paid for furniture peeled off
and the floor of the nearly paid for house
buckled and the walls leaned and the roof caved

III

one side of his old face is black and smooth
but the other looks as if the flesh had been poured
molten on the bones and had cooled like slag
lustrous bluepocked and with crater cups
like a photograph of the surface of the moon
and the eye is absent and even the eyebrow

IV

at Lewisburg there is coal in the ground
not inexhaustible yet unexhausted
and on top there is coal on the spur tracks
gondolas heaped with it tons upon tons
a share of which was mined by Ben P Jones
who may be seen any day on the slate dump
accompanied by his family of five
winnowing the refuse for nuggets of coal
lest they freeze through the winter approaching

V

the Sayreton miners complained and they said
what with the payrate slashed nearly in half
and what with making just two shifts a week
not much was left after stoppage came out
stoppage for rent on the houses they lived in
for medical care of their families
and a doctor when their women gave birth
the Sayreton bosses replied that the stoppage
was optional . . . a roof over your head
was optional and medicine for your children
optional . . . optional to have a doctor
at the birthing time . . . all this was optional

GOOD SAMARITAN

The Negro walked his shoes out looking for work
and when there was nothing left to eat in his house
he deferentially asked for food
and the charitable city after due
investigation which revealed that he really
had a wife and four children and wasn't just
lying allotted them a sack of flour
and half a pound of salt pork and other

plain substantial foods to be consumed
at the rate of nine cents worth daily per each
adult and four and a half cents worth per child
if the ration was to last the week ...
or they could if they preferred eat well
two days and go hungry five ... that was up to them ...

Now the city out of its profound acquaintance
with Negro nature knew that it wasn't sufficient
simply to feed an idle black however badly
in order to keep him in his proper place
but that his mind should be kept occupied
or rather kept unoccupied by thoughts
disturbing to his happy loyal nature ... nor
should he be allowed to get the idea
that he could eat without working lest he
be spoiled for good ... in order therefore
that he might the better digest the bread
of charity and feel that he had in a way
earned it he was ordered to work two days
a week on the roads in exchange for food
worth considerably less than one day's labor ...
On those days he trudged with other of the city's
beneficiaries five miles out to swing
pick and shovel nine hours in red mud and tough
chert rock and then trudged in again to town ...
sometimes they were lucky enough to ride in
on the back of a truck with a Negro driver
(they never had the impudence to hail a white)
and rest their blisters and run up less
of a hunger ... every mile saved was a biscuit
earned ...
            One hot evening as they were tramping
homewards in their rag-swathed wrecks of shoes
while the white folks' cars went whiffing by
pneumatic and easeful and lulling with waft
of wind in passing within a foot at fifty
a ramshackle truck came by headed toward town
with a Negro at the wheel ... they yelled ... the truck
swerved slowing on the shoulder ... they cut across
the road to jump it ... he last ... clenching
his teeth as he ran on swollen bloody feet ...
LOOK OUT they screamed ... and a fast car hit him

The shattered bundle was picked up from the road
by the other Negroes and stowed in a car
driven by a good white man who had stopped
after the accident to see if he could help
and offered to take him to the hospital
since his car was so much faster than the truck
He sped wide-open into town while his burden
fouled the back-seat cushions with clotting pool
and reek of puke . . . and five minutes later
deposited the Negro unconscious but breathing
in the arms of science at the charity hospital
to furnish some interne a bit of practice . . .

It takes a lot to kill one of the sons
of bitches said the interne on the receiving ward
waggling the fractured limbs of the Negro
to see if the pain would make him come to
and since it didn't deciding not to waste
any anaesthetic on the black bastard . . .

The good white man who had brought the patient in
told the hospital authorities
that the Negro had been struck by a southbound car
with a Florida license . . . woman driving . . .
hadn't stopped . . . hit and run . . . damned outrage . . .
when the car hit the poor nigger it threw
him high in the air . . . lit square on his head . . .
yes he'd tried to get the number . . . was a 3
a 6 and a 4 in it . . . couldn't get it for sure . . .
woman must have been clocking around seventy . . .
If he'd been able to get that number
he sure would turn it in on her because
he believed niggers ought to get a square deal
and he wasn't a man to cover anything up
even if it was a white woman in the wrong . . .
no couldn't say what kind of a car it was
you couldn't tell cars apart any more
might have been a Buick or an Olds . . .
Would he give his name? Well if they'd just as soon
he'd rather not . . . he'd done what he could for
the poor nigger stopping and bringing him in
and messing his car all up . . . and if he gave his name
there was no telling what it'd lead to . . .

some jackleg lawyer might take up the case
and haul him into court and waste his time
but he would call up in a couple of days
and find out if the authorities located
that Florida car . . . and if they did he would
be glad to testify and see that the poor
nigger got justice whatever it cost . . .
and then the good white man left in a hurry . . .

Right after he left the Negro's friends
arrived in the slow truck and hung around
afraid to ask anything but wanting to know
if he was surely dead before they told his wife
and finally one of them sidled up to the window
and asked and the girl said he'd been taken
to the operating room and then she asked
had any one of them got that Florida
license number and they said they didn't
know nothin about no Florida license number
and she said hadn't a Florida car hit him
and they said the white gentleman what hit him
done carried him to the hospital in his car

THE BEST STEEL IN THE WORLD

Light bursts from the tap-hole
the big open hearth furnace tilting over on its rockers
and another heat of rail-steel is on its way
made right
for I've watched it from the first scrap charge
through how it took hot metal
the slag fluffing from the high pot the way it ought to
then smoothing down to a creamy boil
cleansing the fierce blue molten steel beneath

A good heat of steel this one
not like that other

that went dead soft in the furnace
and they tried to kid me that the carbon was holding up
and when they found I wouldn't buy that
they switched tests on me
and I caught them at it
and put on my metallurgist's report what they had tried to pull
and condemned the whole heat
110 tons of bad rail steel I sent to the scrap yard
where it belonged
and the superintendent nearly got fired
He tried to run me out of the mill for that
gave orders that nobody was to give me any information or even
    speak to me
and Charley Gray the melter I caught switching tests told people
what he was going to beat out of me
if he ever caught me outside

That was something to go through
not being spoken to for three weeks by the guys I worked with
and having to run my metallurgist's job right on
but I managed somehow
and one by one the guys began breaking down
the third-helpers started giving me dope
then the second-helpers
and finally the first-helpers even
and a lot of them said I'd been right
because rail steel had to be good
to take what it had to take on the line

The molten steel pours in the ladle
and the helpers shovel ferro-silicon through the hole in the shield
I smell the burning cloth of their face wrappings
hear their sharp breaths as they struggle in the searing heat
the scrape of fast shovels on the cherry-red steel floor

The superintendent is standing beside me
about to say something after all these weeks
Sidelong he smiles at me
(we used to be good friends)
then speaks
"We're not paid to make the best steel in the world"
he says
"but to make a profit"

(Far up the line she whistles for a crossing
the deep IC whistle I used to pick out
as a child half-asleep in my bed
from the Frisco the L&N and the AGS whistles
then she whistles nearer
the all-Pullman Panama Limited tearing down the line
Leaning with the curve the locomotive rips around the shoulder
of a yellow Mississippi hill
the flawed rail we once made
snaps in two
and drivers spinning still the mighty engine is on its back in the
        ditch
while escaping steam cooks the mangled bodies of its crew
and buckled up-ended cars where shriek
the trapped
stretch back along the curve)

ENSLEY, ALABAMA: 1932

The mills are down.
The hundred stacks
are shorn of their drifting fume.
The idle tracks
rust . . .
Smeared red with the dust
of millions of tons of smelted ore
the furnaces loom—
towering, desolate tubes—
smokeless and stark in the sun . . .
Powerhouse cubes
turbines hummed in,
platesteel mains the airblast thrummed in
are quiet, and the sudden roar
of blown-off steam . . .
At night
the needle gleam

where the ladle poured at the pig machine,
the deep smoulder of an iron run
and the spreading light
of molten slag over the sleeping town
are seen
no more
now mills and men are down.

FIRE BY NIGHT

when the burnt black bodies of the homeless
were found in the embers of the Negro church
into which they had crept to sleep on the floor
the wails of the people traveled down the cold wind
and reached the ears of the rich on the mountain
like the distant whistle of a fast train coming

VULCAN AND MARS OVER BIRMINGHAM

Here
banal upon his parapet
the god of work gesticulates aloft
clumsily moulded from ore
of the marvelous mountain. The vermilion cleft
of the highway beneath is not
banal though, exposing the iron-fraught strata.

Blurred
by distance and the haze
of many thousand smokes
the city—born of this mountain—lies

gangling over its ridges and valleys, a tired
child-city, full of aches
and growing pains, unsure of its powerful nature.

Stranger,
down there will yet
spread a city adult, no soft
leechlike urban creature
but essential unto its day. What will be left
after the old antagonist wings overhead is not
revealed though, locked in the iron-fraught future.

BEAUFORT TIDES

Low tide.
The scavenging gulls
scour the reaches of mud.
No slavers ride
at anchor in the roads. Rotting hulls
are drawn up on the shore.

Full stood
the tide here
when through this colonnaded door
into the raw land passed bond and free,
the one in hope leading the other in fear,
chained each to each by destiny.

Not only tide
but time and blood
can turn, can ebb and flow.
Time ebbs, blood flows, the fear
shows in the master's eye while jubilee
bursts from the bondsman's throat.

Now
no shout

rings out.
Neither hopes. Both fear.
What future tide will free
these captives of their history?

JEFFERSON DAVIS INAUGURAL

Capitol Portico: Montgomery, Alabama

A brazen star
marks where his haughty feet were set
who later fled
in womanly disguise while near and far
the vengeful victor spoke in flame
and insult till the broken land was red
not with blood and embers only but with shame

A star inlaid
marks where he postured on the marble for a day
with his people ranged below
and seeking to stay history he bayed
the sun like Joshua
The sun impenitently set
and once more rose on irreversible woe

THE SPECTRE IN PLAIN DAY

The chancred denizens of these foul haunts
Lean out of broken windows and entice
Your boys with frowsy blandishments, thirsty
To drink up their innocence, for men are wise

And sate their appetites on cleanlier flesh,
At least when they are sober. But this goes on
With profit to someone, and will go on,
One knows, while the high stars hold their courses
And the high sheriff winks in the court-house
And the spectre in plain day walks unchallenged
      amongst us.

APPALACHIAN LANDSCAPE

Sick and scrawny lies the land, denuded
Of forest, sapped of fertility,
Gutted of coal, the integument of life
Flayed utterly from it and bleeding
Its last weak pulse away down washes and gullies.

Scrawny and sick on the stoops of their shacks,
Idle, dejected are the folk of this land.
One sometimes observes them crawling
About their irremediable fields or plodding
Unwashed homewards from their failing mines.

VEX NOT THIS GHOST

Deep in the moss-draped woods you come upon it,
A ruined church where the first rice-planters worshipped,
Herding their wild Africans into the choir-loft
While in blessed Christian unity master and slave

Devoutly drowsed through the Anglican sermon.
Oddly confounded with a symbol of liberty,
The church first was burned by the redcoats.
Restored by African craftsmen it sweetly resounded
With lauds and rhetoric for three generations
Only to flame up again when the Yankees
Laid their torch to all bulwarks of slavery.
The freed Africans were not so attached
As they had formerly seemed to the genteel rites
Of supervised worship, preferring to clap
And shout by themselves, while their old masters lacked
Skill and lacked heart to rebuild, so they left these walls
Roofless in the live-oaks, and their forbears' graves.

LIKE JUDAS, WASN'T IT?

John Lewis
you don't know who I am
but I've known you
for a long, long time.
I wasn't surprised
John Lewis
when I heard your voice
phony as the herb doctor's in the medicine show
trying to sell the American people
a product
every bit as bogus
as the snake oil
the herb doctor ballyhooed
when I was a kid
on payday in the steel mills—
"Step right up, gents!"
—and the poor working stiffs
Italians from the open hearth pit
Negroes from the slag hole

foundrymen millwrights ingot chasers mixer men and steel pourers
guys with double ruptures
from lifting too much
guys with TB's
from working 13 hour night shifts in the heat and cold
stepped right up to the herb doctor
and laid a buck on the line
for a miraculous bottle of snake oil
"Guaranteed to cure everything that ails you."
John Lewis
eight long years ago
I found out
you were a quack
and when you started the CIO
and guys I believed in
said you had changed and got real
I hoped you had
but I didn't believe you could.
Now you are back at the old stand
bellowing the old ballyhoo
peddling the same old snake oil
in a new bottle
and the label reads
"Wendell L. Willkie, of course!"

In 1932
a guy named Sam Insull
that Willkie thinks a lot of—
what fancy thing did he call him?
"a powerful and appealing figure"—
I think that was it.
Well, this guy Insull
was running Chicago
and also running the State of Illinois
(that was before he skipped off to Greece
to keep out of jail)
and he owned just about everything there was to own
including a great big coal company.
Now this big company like all the other big companies
in Hoover's day
kept cutting wages.
Finally

the Illinois miners decided
to put a stop to it.
They wouldn't sign the contract with Insull's company
cutting wages again.
They said no.
They said they'd starve first.
But you, John Lewis, you told them they had to sign,
they had to take the wage cuts.
I guess you must have agreed with Wendell.
You must have found Sam Insull
"a powerful and appealing figure."
Your miners thought then
and they told me
Sam Insull had an "in" to you, John Lewis.
Maybe you were just a sucker for him.
He made plenty people suckers in his time.
"Sign the contract!" you told your boys
and when they wouldn't
you signed the contract for them.
"Papa knows best!"

The Illinois miners
pulled out of your union
and struck Insull's mines
and you and Insull
and the Governor of Illinois
played ball together.
Sam Insull
fixed the newspapers and put up the dough.
The Governor of Illinois
declared martial law
and called out the National Guard.
You, John Lewis,
furnished the finks and the strikebreakers
by the trainload.
And still the three of you, big as you were
—Sam Insull, the Governor of Illinois and John Lewis—
never could break that strike.
I was in there
at Christmas time '32
and there weren't any Christmas trees
in the miners' houses

and they were burning wood in their coal stoves
and their windows stayed shut
night and day
to keep the little heat in
and the little bombs out
the thugs
had the habit
of heaving into any open windows
just for fun.

I never could forget all that
and I couldn't forget the mass-meetings
and the guys with bloody bandaged heads
and an Italian with an accordion
who sang songs he made up about you, John Lewis,
and they weren't complimentary.
The miners took them up and sang them
on the picket lines they sang them
and they were damn well clubbed for singing them, John Lewis.

Like I say, John Lewis,
I have a long memory
and when guys I believed in
started believing in you
I was sorry for them
because I knew
I just about knew
some day
they were in for
a hell of a big disappointment.
And on the 25th day of October, 1940,
they got it.
Boy, they got it!
Like I say, I wasn't surprised.
But they were.
I'd like to know
how many of the guys that believe in you
listened to you that night
and couldn't believe, John Lewis,
that you were the guy
they had been believing in
and afterwards
went out and got stinking drunk.

I'd like to know
how many guys had to get stinking drunk
to stand what you did.

Let me tell you
about where I heard you.
I was at a union meeting
CIO
and there were whites and Negroes there
guys that worked with their hands
and had worked with their hands
all their lives
not like your pal Wendell
that tried it a little while
just to say he'd done it
and then went to work
on the rest of us.

Well
it was just a union meeting
like any other union meeting
old business
new business
how to stop the boss from frisking them on overtime
election of shop stewards
and then came nine o'clock.
They had a radio in the hall
and the organizer got up
and he said
"Now we will listen to our leader, John Lewis"
and, John Lewis, I wish you could have seen
those faces, believing in you when you started.
I wish you could have seen
those faces change when you got going.
God, if ever I speak to people
and their faces change like those faces changed
I'll go out and hang myself—like Judas, wasn't it?
John Lewis
if you could have seen those faces
when you got through . . .

THE ODYSSEY OF THOMAS BENJAMIN HARRISON HIGGENBOTTOM

Way back when I was young the land was new.
I taken the habit of cleaning it up
for people. Leased me a farm from an Indian
when I got married. We made out all right.
We couldn't complain. Of course we taken fever
and chills. Next farm we rented over by Slick,
but they struck oil on it and put us off.
Good river bottom land I farmed on next,
belonging to a banker. I cleaned it up
and then we moved to Kansas. My wife's folks
lived there. Some wheat growers come in and fenced
the open range. We sold our stock and moved
on back to Oklahoma, figuring
we might do better in country that we knew.
We found a place close to Muskogee
and made a bumper crop, the best there was
in all that neighborhood, then moved again
to Tahlequah and stayed two years. Found me
a bigger farm and bought it from the bank.
Most of that country then was open range.
Got me a bunch of high-class cattle. That
is where the drought first caught us. If I
could just look forward like I do backwards!
To quiet the mortgage on my stock I sold
some cattle off, ten dollars for each cow
I'd paid a hundred for. I owed the bank
a little land note so I sold two hounds,
two running hounds, for a hundred sixty-five.
Two hounds brought more than sixteen head of cattle!
We stayed five years before we sold that farm
and bought a larger one. We made the best
and biggest corn and cotton crop in all
that country our first year but when we left
after four years I owed the bank five hundred
and all I had was three old mules, a pony,
and not one cow. I did have family though,
six boys and these two girls. Now this boy here,
he's going on twelve. Three years ago we left
our place in Oklahoma. Young as he was

I used to put him out behind a mule.
These girls plowed too. I start them young. We work
together. Out in the field my shadow amounts
to a whole lot. You ask them if it don't.
The girls when they come in at noon would grab
their hoes and tend the flower garden. Shore,
my girls did that when they were resting up
from busting out a field. We moved from there
to Wagoner County and took our debts along.
The bank was real obliging, turned me loose
but held me tight. The Wagoner bank took over.
We made a crop but lightning killed two mules
one night and then a cyclone hit through there.
It scared my horse so bad he run into
a tree and broke his neck. That left one mule.
I went to buying scrub stock then for ten
and fifteen dollars. I'd got down to where
my credit wasn't any good because
all my security was gone. About
that time the plow-up come. I told the man
the truth. Generally I raised forty
acres of cotton, sometimes fifty, had
the cotton hands in family for the work
and growing all the living that we had
to have. They caught the feller told the truth
and cut his acres down. I landed with
sixteen instead of forty. When they done that
the older children said, "No use for us
to stay on here. We'll have to hunt a job."
Two of them left. We never heard from them.
That fall we druv the truck to Texas, caught
the cotton picking, made expenses, come
back home no better off. So I put in
for one of them new farm security loans.
We had a bunch of chickens, milk cows and hogs
but we was short on feed. That winter was
real cold. Three hundred of my chickens starved.
You could go out and see them dropping dead.
We lost one mule, one cow, just on starvation.
You know, to a farmer that don't look good.
We got our government loan but not in time.
If I had got that loan to have bought feed
the first of January I could have put

them chickens to producing and went on.
So I says, "Well, now, this is our last crop.
I'll never see another thing of mine
die of starvation, not if I starve to death."
I made my crop, sold out—don't owe no banks—
paid up the government loan, and still had left
a dollar or two. We took a notion then
to leave, one morning loaded up some stuff,
eight head of us—six chaps and two grown folks—
into a roadster, Model A. We'd heard
that Gilbert, Arizona, was the place
where cotton really grew and you could make
good money in the fields, so we took off
down Sixty-six, through Amarillo, Texas,
and was it cold! December was the month.
We got to Gilbert but it wasn't like
they said. We lived in tents, right on the ground.
Them small-poxers, scabby as goats, would come
out in the field and pick. This girl caught it.
Her head was a solid scab. Here comes this school
feller. "She's got to be in school. You see
she's there tomorrow or it's jail for you."
We used to keep them out once in a while
to pick and help get up the grocery bill.
Here comes the health department bringing her back.
"Why did you send that girl to school? Don't you
know smallpox when you see it?" I told him why
I sent her. "Now the school is quarantined,
and this camp too. Nobody better leave."
They kept us quarantined for three whole weeks.
We couldn't even pick. They had to feed us.
When we got loose we went to Avondale
to pick. A barracks made of tin all full
of holes, that was our home, eight people in
one room. Early one morning my wife waked up.
She saw the next room through a great big hole.
A woman there was busy picking lice
off of her children. We got out and come
to California, to the government camp
at Calpat in the Imperial Valley. We
had showers. Things was all kept clean. We stayed
till that camp moved and then we moved with it.
We worked a while in peas best way we could.

Fifteen hundred people just in one field.
They wanted to pick peas so bad they'd fight
over a row. A hamper was the most
I ever picked. No one could live on that.
We went to Beaumont for the cherries. Then
we went up north to Thornton, worked in hay
a little, apricots in San Jose,
and back again to Thornton for tomatoes.
The Filipinos and Japanese
got all the good tomatoes which I guess
they knew how better than the average.
Visalia was the next place. There we chopped
cotton a while and then we tried Calpat
once more. I made hampers. When work give out
we went on back to Thornton. Here a while,
then some place else. We just keep moving on.
You reckon there's a home for us somewhere?
Somebody must could use a family.

ALTOGETHER SINGING

Dream of people altogether singing
each singing his way to self
to realms on realms within
all singing their way on out of self
singing through to unity
kindling into flame of common purpose from the
     altogether singing

such singing once I heard
where black children sang the chants of work in slavery
of hope for life at last and justice beyond the spaded
     unmarked grave
the platform dignitaries
of master race stooping for the occasion
were suddenly shamed and shaken

by these fierce and singing children
chanting out their stormy hunger
for freeborn rights
still wickedly denied

again once
in packed and stifling union hall
where miners gathered and their womenfolk
I heard such singing
while outside in the listening street
men stood uneasy and shivering beneath their heavy
    uniforms
more firmly gripped their guns
though unarmed were the singers
save for the weapon of song

and once again
where followers of the ripening crops
along that hot relentless valley hemmed by cool mirage
    of high Sierras
square danced with riotous feet
outstamping fiddlesqueak and banjo's tinny jingle
there came a quiet
and from the quiet
burst altogether singing
yearning back to lands whence these were driven
the known and homely acres
then lusting forward to the richness of unending rows
    and vines and groves
the treasure tended only
but some day to be taken and be rightly used
the prophecy sang forth

II

IN
EGYPT
LAND

A Narrative Poem,
1940

IN EGYPT LAND

I

It was Alabama, 1932
but the spring came
same as it always had.
A man just couldn't help believing
this would be a good year for him
when he saw redbud and dogwood everywhere in bloom
and the peachtree blossoming
all by itself
up against the gray boards of the cabin.
A man had to believe
so Cliff James hitched up his pair of old mules
and went out and plowed up the old land
the other man's land but he plowed it
and when it was plowed it looked new again
the cotton and corn stalks turned under
the red clay shining with wet
under the sun.

Years ago
he thought he bought this land
borrowed the money to pay for it
from the furnish merchant in Notasulga
big white man named Mr Parker
but betwixt the interest and the bad times coming
Mr Parker had got the land back
and nigh on to $500 more owing to him
for interest seed fertilize and rations
with a mortgage on all the stock—
the two cows and their calves
the heifer and the pair of old mules—
Mr Parker could come drive them off the place any day
if he took a notion
and the law would back him.

Mighty few sharecroppers
black folks or white

ever got themselves stock like Cliff had
they didn't have any cows
they plowed with the landlord's mule and tools
they didn't have a thing.
Took a heap of doing without
to get your own stock and your own tools
but he'd done it
and still that hadn't made him satisfied
The land he plowed
he wanted to be his.
Now all come of wanting his own land
he was back to where he started.
Any day
Mr Parker could run him off
drive away the mules the cows the heifer and the calves
to sell in town
take the wagon the plow tools the store-bought furniture and the
     shotgun
on the debt.
No
that was one thing Mr Parker never would get a hold of
not that shotgun . . .

Remembering that night last year
remembering the meeting
in the church he and his neighbors always went to
deep in the woods
and when the folks weren't singing or praying or clapping and
     stomping
you could hear the branch splashing over rocks
right out behind.
That meeting night
the preacher prayed a prayer
for all the sharecroppers
white and black
asking the good Lord Jesus
to look down
and see how they were suffering.
"Five cent cotton Lord
and no way Lord for a man to come out.
Fifty cents a day Lord for working in the field
just four bits Lord for a good strong hand
from dawn to dark Lord from can till can't

ain't no way Lord a man can come out.
They's got to be a way Lord show us the way . . ."
And then they sang.
"Go Down Moses" was the song they sang
"Go Down Moses, way down in Egypt land
Tell old Pharaoh to let my people go"
and when they had sung the song
the preacher got up and he said
"Brothers and sisters
we got with us tonight
a colored lady teaches school in Birmingham
going to tell us about the Union
what's got room for colored folks and white
what's got room for all the folks
that ain't got no land
that ain't got no stock
that ain't got no something to eat half the year
that ain't got no shoes
that raises all the cotton
but can't get none to wear
'cept old patchedy overhauls and floursack dresses.
Brothers and sisters
listen to this colored lady from Birmingham
who the Lord done sent I do believe
to show us the way . . ."

Then the colored lady from Birmingham
got up and she told them.
She told them how she was raised on a farm herself
a sharecrop farm near Demopolis
and walked six miles to a one-room school
and six miles back every day
till her people moved to Birmingham
where there was a high school for colored
and she went to it.
Then she worked in white folks' houses
and saved what she made
to go to college.
She went to Tuskegee
and when she finished
got a job teaching school in Birmingham
but she never could forget
the people she was raised with

the sharecrop farmers
and how they had to live.
No
all the time she was teaching school
she thought about them
what could she do for them
and what could they do for themselves.
Then one day
somebody told her about the Union . . .
If everybody joined the Union she said
a good strong hand would get what he was worth
a dollar (Amen sister)
instead of fifty cents a day.
At settling time the cropper could take his cotton to the gin
and get his own fair half and the cotton seed
instead of the landlord hauling it off and cheating on the weight.
"All you made was four bales Jim" when it really was six
(Ain't it God's truth?)
and the Union would get everybody the right to have a garden spot
not just cotton crowded up to the house
and the Union would see the children got a schoolbus
like the white children rode in every day
and didn't have to walk twelve miles.
That was the thing
the children getting to school
(Amen)
the children learning something besides chop cotton and pick it
(Yes)
the children learning how to read and write
(Amen)
the children knowing how to figure
so the landlord wouldn't be the only one
could keep accounts
(Preach the Word sister).

Then the door banging open against the wall
and the Laws in their lace boots
the High Sheriff himself
with his deputies behind him.
Folks scrambling to get away
out the windows and door
and the Laws' fists going *clunk clunk clunk*
on all the men's and women's faces they could reach

and when everybody was out and running
the pistols going off behind them.
Next meeting night
the men that had them brought shotguns to church
and the High Sheriff got a charge of birdshot in his body
when Ralph Gray with just his single barrel
stopped a car full of Laws
on the road to the church
and shot it out with their 44's.
Ralph Gray died
but the people in the church
all got away alive.

    II

The crop was laid by.
From now till picking time
only the hot sun worked
ripening the bolls
and men rested after the plowing and plowing
women rested
little boys rested
and little girls rested
after the chopping and chopping with their hoes.
Now the cotton was big.
Now the cotton could take care of itself from the weeds
while the August sun worked
ripening the bolls.

Cliff James couldn't remember ever making a better crop
on that old red land
he'd seen so much of
wash down the gullies toward the Tallapoosa
since he'd first put a plow to it.
Never a better crop
but it had taken the fertilize
and it had taken work
fighting the weeds
fighting the weevils . . .
Ten bales it looked like it would make
ten good bales when it was picked
a thousand dollars worth of cotton once
enough to pay out on seed and fertilize and furnish for the season
and the interest and something down

on the land
new shoes for the family to go to church in
work shirts and overalls for the man and boys
a bolt of calico for the woman and girls
and a little cash money for Christmas.

Now though
ten bales of cotton
didn't bring what three used to.
Two hundred and fifty dollars was about what his share of this
    year's crop would bring
at five cents a pound
not even enough to pay out on seed and fertilize and furnish for
    the season
let alone the interest on the land Mr Parker was asking for
and $80 more on the back debt owing to him.
Mr Parker had cut his groceries off at the commissary last month
and there had been empty bellies in Cliff James' house
with just cornbread buttermilk and greens to eat.
If he killed a calf to feed his family
Mr Parker could send him to the chain-gang
for slaughtering mortgaged stock.

Come settling time this fall
Mr Parker was going to get every last thing
every dime of the cotton money
the corn
the mules
the cattle
and the law would back him.
Cliff James wondered
why had he plowed the land in the spring
why had he worked and worked his crop
his wife and children alongside him in the field
and now pretty soon
they would all be going out again
dragging their long sacks
bending double in the hot sun
picking Mr Parker's cotton for him.

Sitting on the stoop of his cabin
with his legs hanging over the rotten board edges
Cliff James looked across his fields of thick green cotton

to the woods beyond
and a thunderhead piled high in the south
piled soft and white like cotton on the stoop
like a big day's pick
waiting for the wagon
to come haul it to the gin.

On the other side of those woods
was John McMullen's place
and over yonder just east of the woods
Ned Cobb's and beyond the rise of ground
Milo Bentley lived that was the only new man
to move into the Reeltown section that season.
Milo just drifted in from Detroit
because his work gave out up there
and a man had to feed his family
so he came back to the farm
thinking things were like they used to be
but he was finding out different.
Yes
everybody was finding out different
Cliff and John and Ned and Milo and Judson Simpson across the
     creek
even white croppers like Mr Sam and his brother Mr Bill
they were finding out.
It wasn't many years ago Mr Sam's children
would chunk at Cliff James' children
on their way home from school
and split little Cliff's head open with a rock once
because his daddy was getting too uppity
buying himself a farm.
Last time they had a Union meeting though at Milo Bentley's place
who should show up but Mr Sam and Mr Bill
and asked was it only for colored
or could white folks join
because something just had to be done
about the way things were.
When Cliff told them
it was for all the poor farmers
that wanted to stick together
they paid their nickel to sign up
and their two cents each for first month's dues
and they said they would try to get

more white folks in
because white men and black
were getting beat with the same stick these days.

Things looked worse than they ever had in all his time of life
Cliff James thought
but they looked better too
they looked better than they ever had in all his time of life
when a sharecropper like Ralph Gray
not drunk but cold sober
would stand off the High Sheriff with birdshot
and get himself plugged with 44's
just so the others at the meeting could get away
and after that the mob hunting for who started the Union
beating men and women up with pistol butts and bull whips
throwing them in jail and beating them up more
but still not stopping it
the Union going on
more people signing up
more and more every week
meeting in houses on the quiet
nobody giving it away
and now white folks coming in too.

Cliff James looked over his ripening cotton to the woods
and above the trees the thunderhead piled still higher in the south
white like a pile of cotton on the stoop
piling up higher and higher
coming out of the south
bringing storm . . .

III
"You"
Cliff James said
"nor the High Sheriff
nor all his deputies
is gonna git them mules."
The head deputy put the writ of attachment back in his inside
        pocket
then his hand went to the butt of his pistol
but he didn't pull it.
"I'm going to get the High Sheriff and help"

he said
"and come back and kill you all in a pile."

Cliff James and Ned Cobb watched the deputy whirl the car around
and speed down the rough mud road.
He took the turn skidding
and was gone.
"He'll be back in a hour" Cliff James said
"if'n he don't wreck hisseff."
"Where you fixin' to go?" Ned Cobb asked him.
"I's fixin' to stay right where I is."
"I'll go git the others then."
"No need of eve'ybody gittin' kilt" Cliff James said.
"Better gittin' kilt quick
than perishin' slow like we been a'doin' " and Ned Cobb
     was gone
cutting across the wet red field full of dead cotton plants
and then he was in the woods
bare now except for the few green pines
and though Cliff couldn't see him
he could see him in his mind
calling out John McMullen and telling him about it
then cutting off east to Milo Bentley's
crossing the creek on the foot-log to Judson Simpson's . . .
Cliff couldn't see him
going to Mr Sam or Mr Bill about it
no
this was something you couldn't expect white folks to get in on
even white folks in your Union.

There came John McMullen out of the woods
toting that old musket of his.
He said it went back to Civil War days
and it looked it
but John could really knock a squirrel off a limb
or get a running rabbit with it.
"Here I is" John said
and "What you doin' 'bout you folks?"
"What folks?"
"The ones belongin' to you.
You chilrens and you wife."
"I disremembered 'em" Cliff James said.

"I done clean disremembered all about my chilrens and my wife."
"They can stay with mine" John said.
"We ain't gonna want no womenfolks nor chilrens
not here we ain't."

Cliff James watched his family going across the field
the five backs going away from him
in the wet red clay among the dead cotton plants
and soon they would be in the woods
his wife
young Cliff
the two girls
and the small boy . . .
They would just have to get along
best way they could
because a man had to do
what he had to do
and if he kept thinking about the folks belonging to him
he couldn't do it
and then he wouldn't be any good to them
or himself either.
There they went into the woods
the folks belonging to him gone
gone for good
and they not knowing it
but he knowing it
yes God
he knowing it well.

When the head deputy got back
with three more deputies for help
but not the High Sheriff
there were forty men in Cliff James' cabin
all armed.
The head deputy and the others got out of the car
and started up the slope toward the cabin.
Behind the dark windows
the men they didn't know were there
sighted their guns.
Then the deputies stopped.
"You Cliff James!" the head deputy shouted
"come on out

we want to talk with you."
No answer from inside.
"Come on out Cliff
we got something we want to talk over."
Maybe they really did have something to talk over
Cliff James thought
maybe all those men inside
wouldn't have to die for him or he for them . . .
"I's goin' out" he said.
"No you ain't" Ned Cobb said.
"Yes I is" Cliff James said
and leaning his shotgun against the wall
he opened the door just a wide enough crack
for himself to get through
but Ned Cobb crowded in behind him
and came out too
without his gun
and shut the door.
Together they walked toward the Laws.
When they were halfway Cliff James stopped
and Ned stopped with him
and Cliff called out to the Laws
"I's ready to listen white folks."

"This is what we got to say nigger!"
and the head deputy whipped out his pistol.
The first shot got Ned
and the next two got Cliff in the back
as he was dragging Ned to the cabin.
When they were in the shooting started from inside
everybody crowding up to the windows
with their old shotguns and muskets
not minding the pistol bullets from the Laws.
Of a sudden John McMullen
broke out of the door
meaning to make a run for his house
and tell his and Cliff James' folks
to get a long way away
but a bullet got him in the head
and he fell on his face
among the dead cotton plants
and his life's blood soaked into the old red land.

The room was full of powder smoke and men groaning
that had caught pistol bullets
but not Cliff James.
He lay in the corner quiet
feeling the blood run down his back and legs
but when somebody shouted
"The Laws is runnin' away!"
he got to his feet and went to the door and opened it.
Sure enough three of the Laws
were helping the fourth one into the car
but it wasn't the head deputy.
There by the door-post was John McMullen's old musket
where he'd left it when he ran out and got killed.
Cliff picked it up and saw it was still loaded.
He raised it and steadied it against the door-post
aiming it at where the head deputy would be sitting
to drive the car.
Cliff only wished
he could shoot that thing like John McMullen . . .

    IV

He didn't know there was such a place in all Alabama
just for colored.
They put him in a room to himself
with a white bed and white sheets
and the black nurse put a white gown on his black body
after she washed off the dried black blood.
Then the black doctor came
and looked at the pistol bullet holes in his back
and put white bandages on
and stuck a long needle in his arm
and went away.

How long ago was it
he stayed and shot it out with the Laws?
Seemed like a long time
but come to think of it
he hid out in Mr Sam's corn crib
till the sun went down that evening
then walked and walked all the night-time
and when it started to get light he saw a cabin
with smoke coming out the chimney
but the woman wouldn't let him in to get warm

so he went on in the woods and lay down
under an old gum tree and covered himself with leaves
and when he woke up it was nearly night-time again
and there were six buzzards perched in the old gum tree
watching him . . .
Then he got up and shooed the buzzards away
and walked all the second night-time
and just as it was getting light
he was here
and this was Tuskegee
where the Laws couldn't find him
but John McMullen was dead in the cotton field
and the buzzards would be at him by now
if nobody hadn't buried him
and who would there be to bury him
with everybody shot or run away or hiding?

In a couple of days it was going to be Christmas
yes Christmas
and nobody belonging to Cliff James
was going to get a thing
not so much as an orange or a candy stick
for the littlest boy.
What kind of a Christmas was that
when a man didn't even have a few nickels
to get his children some oranges and candy sticks
what kind of a Christmas and what kind of a country anyway
when you made ten bales of cotton
five thousand pounds of cotton
with your own hands
and your wife's hands
and all your children's hands
and then the Laws came to take your mules away
and drive your cows to sell in town
and your calves
and your heifer
and you couldn't even get commissary credit
for coffee molasses and sow-belly
and nobody in your house had shoes to wear
or any kind of fitting Sunday clothes
and no Christmas for nobody . . .
"Go Down Moses" was the song they sang
and when they had finished singing

it was so quiet in the church
you could hear the branch splashing over rocks
right out behind.
Then the preacher got up and he preached . . .

"And there was a man what fought to save us all
he wropped an old quilt around him
because it was wintertime and he had two pistol bullets in his back
and he went out of his house
and he started walking across the country to Tuskegee.
He got mighty cold
and his bare feet pained him
and his back like to killed him
and he thought
here is a cabin with smoke coming out the chimley
and they will let me in to the fire
because they are just poor folks like me
and when I have got warm
I will be on my way to Tuskegee
but the woman was afeared
and barred the door again him
and he went and piled leaves over him in the woods
waiting for the night-time
and six buzzards settled in an old gum tree
watching did he still breathe . . ."

The Sheriff removed Cliff James from the hospital to the county jail on December 22. A mob gathered to lynch the prisoner on Christmas day. For protection he was taken to jail in Montgomery. Here Cliff James died on the stone floor of his cell, December 27, 1932.

III

AND I WILL
BE HEARD
Two Talks to the
American People,
1940

I

AND I WILL BE HEARD

I

When Abraham Lincoln wasn't more than a kid
a man by the name of William Lloyd Garrison
got an idea.

This idea of his was
that slavery had to go.
Now plenty of people agreed with this Garrison
even some people who owned slaves themselves—
they thought slavery wasn't right,
and they said so to people they knew real well
and argued and talked around a little bit
like you do.
All except Garrison.

Garrison put what he thought in the paper.
A little paper that he owned himself
and called the Liberator.
You see, the big papers then even in the North
were owned by folks that were getting something out of slavery
or thought they were.
Naturally, they wouldn't print Garrison's stuff.
No, of course not.
They not only wouldn't print it
but they smeared him for saying the things he did
in his little old paper the Liberator
which didn't have many readers
and no advertisers.
You wouldn't have thought they'd have paid him any mind
no more than you would
some kind of little bug
buzzing around
but he must have bothered them a lot
judging by the way they slapped and swatted at him.

First they said he was an agitator
a dangerous man
who was getting people all excited
about nothing.
But Garrison just kept on putting out his paper
saying slavery was a crime
and had to go.
He just kept pouring it on.

And it must have burned the right people
because pretty soon they had him in jail.
They pinned a libel conviction on him.
He named a New England ship-owner in his paper
and said he was moving more slaves into the South in his ships
which was against the law of the land.
But the courts of the land
put Garrison in jail
instead of the ship-owner.
Funny how it goes some times.

But this was mighty dumb business
for Garrison's enemies to pull
because framing a guy for something
that isn't really a crime
or that he never did at all
when what you've really got against him
is what he thinks—
the ideas he has in his head—
that's dumb
that's worse than dumb.
You can lock up a man
but not his ideas.
You can even kill a man
and his ideas will live.
The only way to kill an idea
is to fight it with a better one.

So Garrison came out of jail
with the same ideas that he went in with
only stronger
and tougher.
A jail is a good quiet place to get your ideas worked out in.
When Garrison got free

he started up his little paper the Liberator again
and he said
"I am in earnest"—
and he said
"I will not equivocate"—
(meaning that he would not say slavery was on the one hand bad
but on the other hand good depending on how you looked at it
which was the way the politicians were mostly talking then
just as they are now)
and he said
"I will not retreat a single inch"—
"And I will be heard"
he said.

My name is John Beecher
and I am writing this piece
mainly about what goes on inside of me
and what I am thinking on May 22, 1940
when the invasion from Mars has really started
that everybody laughed about
when some poor suckers
everywhere
were taken in by the radio play
and believed it was true
and how we laughed
and laughed at them
but now the laugh is on us.

First, though, about me.
You have got to know my genealogy.
Not because it is important
but because a lot of people in authority seem to think so these days.
The thoughts inside my head at the moment
and the feelings burning me up
might disturb some of the authorities, if they knew.
They don't, so they should be told.
Nobody knows except me, so I will tell them.

I don't know how many thousands of family lines
I come down through.
I doubt whether anybody knows all that about himself
except perhaps some King
if there is a King left anywhere tonight.

(I missed the last news broadcast.)
I'll just tell what I know.
I think it was exactly 303 years ago that a certain John Beecher
just an ordinary guy from some little town in England
landed on the shore of Massachusetts Bay
near what was going to be Boston.
He didn't have anything.
No money, education, or anything like that, no aristocratic title.
Just a migrant.
Just looking for a job to keep himself and his wife and kid
like the Okies that John Steinbeck writes about in California today.
A new deal was what that John Beecher was looking for
a start
a toe-hold in the new world.
He didn't find anything in Massachusetts Bay
so after his first year there
he and six other men
just ordinary guys like himself who weren't much
but were willing to work and could take it
pushed on down the coast
and started them a colony called Connecticut.
They knew it was going to be tough, so they left their families
    behind.
Just seven men, and a winter to get through in a hut they built.
Just seven men, and they decided to be a town, and they called it
    New Haven.

The winter turned out to be tough, tougher than they thought.
They were cold in the hut.
They had mighty little to eat.
Indians pestered them.
John Beecher didn't make it.
He died.
The history book doesn't tell what he died from.
Indians, maybe, or froze to death or starved.
John Beecher wasn't important.
Just one man out of seven.
New Haven went on.

I nearly missed out being an American
or even a human being at all
because John Beecher's widow who had been left behind in Massa-
    chusetts Bay

with her little boy
felt there wasn't much left in America for her
with John gone.
She wanted to go on back to England
to the little country town wherever it was they came from
but the other colonists finally persuaded her to stay.
She was a midwife.
They expected to have babies in New Haven.
They would need to have them if they were going to fill up the place
and really get to be a town not just the name of one
and really be the colony of Connecticut.

John Beecher's widow went to New Haven with her little boy
she was the town midwife
she helped the mothers get the babies born
and the town grew.
Her boy learned a trade
blacksmithing was it
because a town had to have a blacksmith
to make all the iron things people used then
like plows to raise their food
pots to cook it in
hammers to build their houses
and guns.

This Beecher was a good blacksmith
and so was his son
and his son's son
and from father to son
for I don't know how many generations
the Beechers were the blacksmiths
in New Haven.
There was one in 1650.
There was still one in 1776
and some Governor said he was the best blacksmith in New England.
I don't know about that.
I do know that he made a lot of guns
when guns were needed
to shoot the enemies of America.

At Bunker Hill
(Wait till you see the whites of their eyes)
his guns got redcoats.

At Valley Forge
(when American soldiers starved and watched American farmers
drive past
in the valley beneath
with wagonloads of grain and pork and beef toward Philadelphia
where the British army was and could pay for it in gold and not
paper money put out by the American Continental Congress—
"not worth a Continental")
I say at Valley Forge
the starving, freezing soldiers
who didn't desert
but stuck by Washington
walked their posts, some of them,
with Beecher guns on their shoulders.
And at Yorktown at last
when Cornwallis surrendered
and the war was won
and America was,
Beecher guns
presented arms.

In 1796
the first Beecher
finished college.
Lyman his name was
and the college was Yale
not much of a place it was then
no money
no fine buildings
and all the students
worked their way through.

This Lyman was a poor preacher
but even if he was a poor preacher
he had the guts to raise a family.
Yes, he went on having kids
when he ought to have known he couldn't support them
or give them advantages and this and that
and he had thirteen
and eight of them were famous
in their day.

One of Lyman's kids
was a girl named Harriet

and she married a poor preacher like her dad was
and his name was Calvin Stowe.
That made her name Harriet Beecher Stowe.
Before she was married
her dad was head of a theological school
where they trained preachers
on the Ohio River outside of Cincinnati.
That was before the Civil War
and to keep from having a war
and to keep from doing anything about slavery
the North and the South had made a deal
called the "Fugitive Slave Law."
It said
that if a slave got away from his master down South
and managed somehow to make his way up without being caught
and finally crossed the Ohio River into the free North
he still was a slave.
You could catch him in Ohio or Michigan or New York
and ship him back to Georgia
where his master
would be waiting for him
with a bull-whip.
Yes, that was the deal.

Now some people up North thought that deal
was the lousiest, dirtiest deal that was ever made in the history of
      the world
and they decided they wouldn't put up with it.
They decided to be rebels.
They decided to break the law.
Lyman Beecher was one of them.
He and some others organized what they called
"The Underground Railroad."
The school for preachers that Lyman was the head of
was one end of the railroad.
The other was in Canada.
When a slave got across the Ohio River
he went to Lyman's school and Lyman hid him out.
Then Lyman passed him up the line and all along the line
other people that had the same idea Lyman had
hid him out.
Finally the slave got to Canada
and when he hit Canada
he wasn't a slave any longer.

As they say these days
Lyman Beecher stuck his neck out.
He broke the Fugitive Slave Law.
His daughter Harriet watched it happen
and she talked to the escaping slaves as they came through
and she got their stories
and she got to feel that all their stories
made one big story
and she wrote it
and she named it
"Uncle Tom's Cabin."

"Uncle Tom's Cabin"
was read by more people
than any book that was ever written
except the Bible.
Not only in America
but all over the world.
It was translated into French, German, Dutch, Swedish, Italian,
        Spanish, Portuguese,
Greek, Hungarian, and I don't know what all other languages.
Millions of people read it
and not so many years later
Abraham Lincoln
said to Harriet Beecher Stowe
"So you are the little lady
who made the great war."

Another one of Lyman's children
was named Henry—
Henry Ward Beecher.
When Henry Ward Beecher finished Amherst College
the president of the college handed him his diploma and said
"Well, this is the last we shall hear of you, Mr. Beecher."
But it wasn't.
When England was ready to go to war against the American Union
to save the Confederacy
to save slavery
but most of all to buy cotton cheap again
why then this Henry Ward Beecher went to England
one man that Amherst College never expected to hear of again
just one man
against what everybody said was England.
And they told him

"Why, you can't talk in Liverpool, Liverpool will murder you"
and
"Don't try to say anything in Manchester, on account of everybody
is out of work
because there isn't any cotton for the mills."
DON'T YOU DARE TO SPEAK, HENRY WARD BEECHER
posters told him on the walls of the towns
and he got threat notes
without any names signed to them
BUT HE SPOKE
YES
HE INSISTED ON SPEAKING.
One place the audience hissed and booed him for half an hour
when he appeared on the stage.
He just stood there and took it, not bothered.
Hissing and booing gets tiresome
to the people who are doing it
so finally they began to quiet down
and when they did
Henry Ward Beecher went to the edge of the stage and squatted
      down
and started talking in a quiet voice to the people in the first row.
Then the second row quit hissing and booing.
They wanted to hear what he was saying.
Then the third row stopped.
Then the fourth.
Then the fifth.
Finally Henry Ward Beecher was talking in a loud voice to every-
      body in the hall
and everybody in the hall was listening.
Yes, listening.
And England did not go to war against the American Union.
And the American Union was saved.

I could tell some more about Lyman Beecher's children but these
      two
were the main ones.
Edward, who was my great-grandfather,
was the first president of the first college in Illinois,
he also wrote books
and was pastor of one of the big churches in Boston.
Catherine believed the women of the country needed education
when most other people thought all they needed
was needlework and how to cook,

but Catherine went to bat
for the American woman's right
to learn.
Isabella worked for woman's suffrage
Charles wrote books and James
raised a regiment of Negro troops
in North Carolina,
then led them as colonel for three years
when the penalty for leading Negro troops against the Confederacy
was, if you were captured,
death.

The youngest one was named Thomas K.
All his life practically he ran a small-town church
and turned down chances
at big-time stuff.
There were seven denominations that had churches in his town
and he wrote a book
"Our Seven Churches"
not knocking a single one
but saying they all
had something.
Also
he was fond of beer
and went for it himself to the brewery
in what I believe they used to call a surrey.
Anyhow it was open like a pick-up truck and the brewery put a keg
    of beer in the back
and Thomas K. drove up the main street
on his way home to the parsonage
so nobody in town could miss knowing
that he drank beer.

My grandfather Frederick Beecher was a Congregational
and then an Episcopal preacher
at Sodus Point on Lake Ontario
and afterwards at Wellsville, New York—
little towns that nobody ever heard of
and nobody ever heard of him
but when he went to New York City
people on the street
thought he was Henry Ward Beecher come back to life
and this made him happy enough.

His son, my father
Leonard Thurlow Beecher
at the age of ten
drew pictures of Erie Railroad engines
which was the only railroad Wellsville was on
and I have looked at these pictures
and if you wanted to make a model of one of those old engines
down to the last detail
including the scroll work on the cab
you could do it
from one of his pictures.

Leonard Thurlow's mother
was named Sarah Hale Goodwin
from Newburyport, Massachusetts.
The Goodwins were sea-captains
who sailed their clippers
to Java and Japan
when Java and Japan
were mighty faraway places.
Mixed with the Goodwins were Hales.
Nathan Hale was one
and the British shot him as a spy
but first he said—
"I regret that I have but one life
to lose for my country."

Edward Everett Hale was another
and he wrote a story called "The Man Without a Country"
about an American who wanted to sell America out
to get something for himself.
This man said—
"God damn the United States"
but God damned him instead.

    II
I think everybody knows
that Henry Ford
has done a lot for this country.
He had an idea
a great idea
and when he was laughed at
he believed in it all the harder

and put it over
and the American people
backed him
and gave him a lot of their money
in the form of profits
to use
because his was the kind of an idea
that took a lot of money
to be worked out.

But then Henry Ford appeared to get
a funny idea
a wrong idea
that this was his money
that he had "made" it himself
and he got another idea
that he knew all the answers
and that "history was bunk."
Now American history is not bunk.
The kind Henry Ford would like to have written is
but not the kind I am writing in this piece.
If the kind of American history I am writing
was bunk
there wouldn't have been any Henry Ford
and he ought to know it.
He used to know it
but lately
he is acting
as if he had forgotten.

Henry Ford says
to the people who work for him
I will treat you better than anybody else will
and pay you more
but you have got to be thankful
and do exactly what I say do
and let me tell you
exactly what to think
whether to take a drink or not
not to join a union
et cetera.
Recently the United States Senate
through one of its committees

heard what was going on
what Henry Ford was up to
having guys' teeth knocked out
for coming around his plants
telling "his" people
they ought to join something
the American law
gives them a right to join
if they want to
but Henry Ford thinks
they oughtn't to
which is all right if he wants to think it
but is not all right
is all wrong
when he tries to stop them
with blackjacks
and if Henry Ford had the sense God gave a june bug
he would know that it wouldn't even work
for very long.

By God Henry Ford
you have got to stop it
you have got to lay off that stuff
and lay off quick
or the American people
who don't belong to you at all
but to whom you yourself belong
are going to teach you a lesson.
They gave you their money
our money
everybody's money
to do something for all of us
that needed doing
and nobody else but you could do.
That money you have got
is a trust
and don't you forget it.

Listen, Henry Ford.
We are hearing a lot these days
about the "Fifth Column"
about "Trojan Horses"
and parachute troops in disguise

who go around with dynamite
and flame-throwers
disrupting communications behind the lines
setting destructive fires
holding strategic bridgeheads
and spreading stories of disaster, which is the worst thing they do.

Pretty soon
I expect you to begin hollering
like you usually do in a crisis
I expect you to begin popping off
and pointing with alarm
and trying to scare everybody half to death
but be careful this time
be mighty careful
or the American people
will get on to you.
We will begin to think
that it is you
that came out of the Trojan Horse
yes you
that came dropping down out of the enemy bomber
in a parachute
disguised as an old woman.

And Charles Augustus Lindbergh
I remember the day
when you
were the American people
brave
invincible
what we all deep down knew we all of us were
and I remember another day
when we all grieved with you
and your child was our child
and we forgave you
when you moved to England
and we understood
why you wanted to be private.
But now
you want to be public again
and you are handing us
some pretty funny stuff.
It is all right to tell us Hitler's bombers won't be here next week

because you are an expert on bombers
and you may know
even though you experts have been wrong all along about Hitler
still you have a right to say what you really think.
But just don't go on from that
to making politics out of it.
Be sure you aren't trying to put ahead some party or other.
Watch it.
We still remember
Hermann Goering pinning a medal on you
and we have a picture in our heads of Hitler looking on
and that day
you could have been the American people again
if you had just quietly told that Hermann Goering
where to shove his medal.

William Randolph Hearst
you are another public character
I feel like saying something to.
Long ago
I stopped reading your lousy papers
and if I did happen to pick one up
the last thing I would turn to
would be your editorials.
I don't know what you are saying at the moment
but you must be getting careful
because otherwise I would be hearing about it from somewhere.
All I want to talk to you about
is an estate you have in California
called San Simeon.
I saw it for the first time last Christmas Eve
driving by on the highway just as dark was coming down
and I didn't know there was such a place in this country
or such brass
as you must have had
to dare build it just for yourself.
Do you know
how the Okies have to live in California
or haven't you bothered to look around?
And those folks whose farms blew away
or were tractored off the land
back in Oklahoma, Texas and Arkansas
have you seen their faces?
I had just come from seeing them

when I drove by your place
San Simeon
on Christmas Eve.
The gall of you
to dare call that place after a disciple of Christ
and to pretend in your newspapers
that you
William Randolph Hearst
are a defender of the Christian faith
against infidels.

John Lewis and Bill Green,
we folks down here have got tired of listening to you squabbling.
You have got to start listening to us for a change
and patch it up quick.
Bill
we hear you have racketeers in some of your unions
and don't do anything about it.
You figure maybe
that it takes racketeers to fight racketeers
and certainly there are more Willie Bioffs
in Palm Beach
than there are in your unions.
It really doesn't take them though.
Have the guts to throw them out.
John
what made you strong a while back
and will make you strong again
is an idea
the unity of labor
one big union for every industry
not just carpenters or plumbers
taking the cream for themselves
and the hell with common labor
but everybody in the same army.
That idea is a whole lot better one
than Bill Green's
an American idea
and it can't help winning.
Just don't get the notion that it is you doing it though
because that is your danger
or that you can do away with democracy
without doing away

with everything.
You are just as strong
as the people back of you
and when they aren't back of you
you are weak.

Earl Browder
you are in jail but I guess you can hear this.
They put you in for traveling under a fake passport
and you belong there.
Yes
You belong there.
When Mr. Stalin said jump you jumped
and tried to kid us into believing
it was Washington and Lincoln who gave you orders.
You were just as phony
as the Daughters of the American Revolution
who also
travel under fake passports.
We once thought you Communists had something
courage
honesty
love of humanity
and that you were really doing something over in Russia
but you sold us out
and don't think for a minute
we're apt to forget it.

And now Martin Dies
Congressman from Texas
you've been running quite a circus up there in Washington
with yourself the star performer.
What you pretended to be doing
investigating un-American activities
was fine and we were all for it
and sometimes you did that
but sometimes you made hay for yourself and Vice President Garner
and smeared folks
that were a lot better Americans than you were, either of you.
How come
Mr. Henry Ford
and Mr. Tom Girdler the head of Republic Steel
haven't been up before your committee?

Adolf Hitler
the Belgian Army has just surrendered to you
and I suppose you feel good about it
but this is the way my little girl Joan Beecher, aged six,
feels about you
and all the other little girls
you have slaughtered
felt before they could write down how they felt:
"When *shell* I come to death?
I am afraid death will come.
And oh I know he looks ugley.
Will my heart have to pear
into his ugley one?
Oh dear, oh dear, is he coming now?
Oh I see him
Yes it is him."

But my little boy Len aged eight
who is going to be a trick airplane pilot when he grows up
and pick up handkerchiefs with his wing-tips
says "Hitler is a sissy."
Yes, that's what he says
and he doesn't care if you hear it, Adolf.
He's got your number, buddy.
He knows you can kill everybody maybe
but you can't really conquer anybody,
least of all Americans.
You
are just setting things up
for us.
When you have killed everybody
you can kill
with everything you can think up to kill with
you will be through
absolutely through
and you yourself will die
in every way there is to die
and you know it yourself
because you said so
before you sent your bombers over
the Joan Beechers of Poland.
Then
we will get going at last.

Yes, we
the Americans
we the people of the new world
will take over
the empire
you tried to found
but your idea
was death
and ours is life
and the thirteen bars in the American flag
will stay thirteen
but the forty-eight stars
will multiply
will get to be
from a constellation
a galaxy
because humanity
will join us.

II

THINK IT OVER, AMERICA

I

This is John Beecher talking to you.
The French government has just finished giving up
to Hitler and Mussolini
and the American people are getting ready to give up
what America stands for
to stop them.
We can stop them all right
and we are going to stop them
but not
by copying Hitler and Mussolini.

I say
America's first line of defense
is in our own backyard.
In March 1933
we started really cleaning up
and all we've managed to do in seven years
is get going on that big job.
Don't believe the baloney
about how the billions for battleships
will leave us so busted
we have got to economize on slum clearance and old age pensions
    and workers' wages.
This is the bunk
and the people who are peddling it
are the same traitors
the same Benedict Arnolds
who ever since 1933
have been saying
we couldn't afford so much relief
we couldn't afford to put a floor under wages and a ceiling over
    hours
we couldn't afford old age pensions

and slum clearance
and all the rest of the New Deal.
I say
we can't afford to stop a single thing
we have started
to make this American democracy we have been talking about ever
     since 1776
come really true.
We have got to step it up.
We have got to give the American people
such a stake in America
they will fight for America
like Washington's men did.

Take some guy
named Bashinsky or Tomburello or Schmidt or maybe Murphy
raised in the slums
of Chicago or Scranton or San Francisco or Savannah or Salem
with one dirty window looking out on a 4 by 4 airshaft
or a blackened wall
or a cobblestone street full of beer trucks and ramshackle streetcars
with never ever enough to eat on the frayed oilcloth in the dark
     kitchen
no milk to build his bones and teeth
vegetables out of cans
rotten meat
and never saw an orange except Christmas.
The ashdump to play on
or back of the billboards on a vacant lot
up and down fire escapes
hanging around the poolhalls.

I say take this guy grown up
named Bashinsky or Tomburello or Schmidt or maybe Murphy
in Chicago or Scranton or San Francisco or Savannah or Salem
off his little job
in the slaughterhouse or coal mine or docks or bag factory or textile
     mill or on the WPA—
Take this guy I say
and put a steel helmet on his head
drape an OD blouse with eagle buttons and padded shoulders
around his bony chest
puttee his bowlegs

and shove a Garand automatic rifle in his hand
give him a sack of grenades
and tell him to go get Hitler.
"Sick 'em, Fido!
Democracy is at stake!"
Who thinks this guy
named Bashinsky or Tomburello or Schmidt or maybe Murphy
is going to think
anything but
Nuts?
What is Hitler to him
what is democracy to him
that he should give a damn which?

II

Gathered Facts about the Brutal killing of Willie Hall.
Shot Friday evening January 12th, 1940 2"45 P.M. by Henry
Collins A white Man serving in the capasity of A Forman
for Mr. H. Chanler big farmer in Belle Glade, Florida.
Willie Hall was a victom of Infantile Paralysis From Infancy
and was about 34 years of age. He earned his own living being
only able to work about five hours a day some time less, the
day he was killed he worked from early morning untill noon.
on his way home in the colored section he was ask if he wanted
to work he stated that he had just come in off the job
Collins said to him you Niggers are just trying to dodge
work got out of his truck advancing toward Willie with a wrecking
bar in his hand Then Willie detecting that Collins was angry
raised the stick that he used to walk with to protect hem-self
then Collins said you wait untill I get back I am going to
kill a nigger today Collins get in his truck to go get a gun
on his return inquired as to where Willie lived the person that
gave Collins this Information no doubt did not know Collins
intentions Collins parked his truck and walked about three
     hundred
feet to the house where Willie was sitting on the stepps resting
had never gone into the house. Collins walked up and said you
think you are one of thouse bad niggers (speaking to a Man that
couldn't eaven walk very far without the aid of a stick) Before
Willie could say one word Collins fired four shots one shot
hitting Willie He fell to the ground his cousin was washing
with in a few feet of Willie She had to run in to the house from

*fright and the posibility of being hit also. Several attempts
were made to get an Oficer of the Law but None could be found for
some time Willie was rushed to the Everglade Memorial Hospital
where He died A few hours later. After every thing had becom
quiet A police Man was found and his reply was that he could
not do anything now. Collins never was Arrested. He was ask
to come to Pahokee in the City of the Hospital for the Inquest
at which time the Justis of the Peace desided the Case as
Justifiable Homerside.
The Negroes were so Aroused over the Brutal killing of Willie
they Employed a white Lawer to Prosecute Collins The Lawer had
Willie's Step Father to Take out A warent for him and the warent
laid Idle for several days before it was served and at that
Collins Never was arrested Neither put in Jail The County Solicitor
did not want the case to come in his courts and Abuse the Lawer
for excepting a case to Prosecute a white Man for killing A nigger
with Fifteen witnesses testifying in the defince of Willie Hall
the Soliciter through the Case out*

Fellow Americans
you never read this story in your newspapers.
Pretty soon though
you will be reading in your newspapers
that Nazi agents
that Reds
are working among the Negroes in the South
organizing them into a Fifth Column
and that it's up to us
to hang the agitators
and put the niggers down.
Then
I hope you will read this story again
and think about it
hard.
The spelling and punctuation aren't all they might be
because the guy that wrote it
was just a Negro tractor driver
without much education.
All he knew how to do
was put down the facts.
Think them over, America.
This sort of business

goes on all the time
and has gone on
ever since the first slave ship touched the American shore.
When
are we going to put a stop to it?
Now I ask you
fair-minded people
loyal Americans
how would you feel about America
if you were a southern Negro
and believed you belonged to the human family
and yet got treated
just like Hitler treats the Jews?

III

Not long ago I was riding the Pennsy
between New York and Washington
and I noticed a kid about 18
in a military school uniform
sitting by himself
and thinking hard about something
and I wanted to know what
so I sat down by him
and asked him.

It wasn't Hitler
he was thinking about
like I expected
because he had on a uniform.
Hitler wasn't bothering him much.
Strange to say
it was the Standard Oil Company
that was on his mind,
and this is how come.

The kid was a Venezuelan
studying in this country.
When he finishes military school
he is going to Penn State
and get to be a dentist
because Venezuela needs dentists
and what he most wants to do in the world
is help Venezuela, his country.

Now what this kid was thinking about so hard was this.
He was on his way back to military school in Virginia
and in a short time they were going to have some exercises
and he was graduating at them
and was what they call
the valedictorian of his class
and had to speak a piece
in front of the cadets and officers and parents and everybody.

The kid had picked out
what he thought was a good piece
a poem by a Venezuelan
called "The Drill"
telling how the Standard Oil Company
takes the oil of Venezuela
and crushes the people of Venezuela who work for it
and corrupts the politicians of Venezuela
so they take orders
from the Standard Oil Company
instead of the people of Venezuela.

The kid had translated this poem called "The Drill"
from Spanish into English
and shown it to his professors
but they said
no no
that was no kind of a piece to speak
at the exercises
in front of the cadets and officers and parents and everybody
no no no no
no kind of a piece at all
to speak.

And the kid couldn't understand.
He thought Americans were pretty swell people
and if they just knew
what the Standard Oil Company
had made America mean
to the people of Venezuela
they would do something about it
they would put a stop
to the Standard Oil Company
wrecking his country.

So
in his small way
he just wanted to start telling
a few Americans
within reach of his voice
so they would get the idea
and pass it on
each one telling it
to the Americans within reach of his voice
and after a while
all the Americans
would have the idea
and would give the Standard Oil Company
the red light at last.

When the kid had finished telling me all this
the train stopped in a station
and he looked out and he asked me
"What place is this?"
and I told him
"Philadelphia"
and I asked him
"You know what Philadelphia means?"
and he nodded his head
and I said "This is where America got going
on July 4, 1776
and we kept on going
and your guy Bolívar down in South America
got the idea from us
and you freed yourselves
and then we proclaimed the Monroe Doctrine
which meant
we were going to keep you free
and we did
for a while.
Then we started pushing you around
because you were too weak
too divided
to stop us
and we called that
the Monroe Doctrine."
The kid nodded his head again.
"When you tried to do something" I went on

"about some American corporation
that was robbing you
an American battleship
showed up in the harbor."
"Yes" he said.
"And when you were under the thumb
of a thieving dictator
like Gomez in your country and Machado in Cuba
guys every bit as bad in every way
as Hitler and Mussolini
and the people tried to throw them off
America
lent the dictators money
to pay their gangsters
to shoot the people down."
"Yes" said the kid.
"But you know" I said
"that the American people
didn't really know what was going on
because their leaders
lied to them
their newspapers
lied to them
it was only the American bankers and big-wigs
that were back of that stuff."
"Yes" he said.
"And if you thought" I said
"if you Latin Americans really knew
that you could trust the United States
that the American people
were for
the people of Venezuela
the people of Brazil
the people of Peru
the people of Mexico even
we could count on you, couldn't we?"
"Yes" he said.

We thought a minute and then I said
"Maybe you and I here in Philadelphia
on May 21, 1940
are starting off something
just as big

as we started off here
on July 4, 1776.
Maybe we are getting this idea of America
going again.
Why did we have to stop
with 48 states?
Wouldn't you folks come into our union
if we asked you in
as equals?"

The kid didn't say yes
and he didn't nod his head
he just looked at me
and looked
and he didn't have to say anything
because I knew he knew
I wasn't just some stranger on the train
handing him some bunk
but the American people talking turkey
and he knew I knew
he wasn't just a kid in a cadet's uniform
but the people of Latin America
wanting to join us
not to save democracy
BUT TO GET DEMOCRACY AT LAST
FOR ALL THE AMERICAN PEOPLES.

IV
Now I am going to come to the point.
Maybe some of you don't see yet
how this piece adds up.
First the stuff about the guy
named Bashinsky or Tomburello or Schmidt or maybe Murphy
next the story about Willie Hall
who got killed because he was black
and his murderer wasn't even arrested
just because he was white
and finally the kid from Venezuela
and what was going on
inside his head.

This is what I mean.
We have got to stop Hitler.

He is the mortal enemy
of everything we believe in
of everything some of us have got
of everything most of us have not got—
that is, liberty
that is, security
that is, democracy
but still believe in
and still believe America will give us.

To stop Hitler
may take a lot of battleships
a lot of airplanes
a lot of Garand automatic rifles
but first and foremost
it will take
American unity.
Now American unity
is not something you get
by clamping down.
That way
is opening the back door
for Hitler
or somebody worse
to walk in.
GET THIS, AMERICA!

The guy
named Bashinsky or Tomburello or Schmidt or maybe Murphy
stands for everybody
ill-housed
ill-clothed
ill-fed
in this rich land of ours.
Would you blame him
if he bit the hand that fed him slops
while real food was being plowed under?
But statesmen warn us of monetary collapse
of exceeding the statutory debt limit
whatever the hell that is
if we try to give this guy a stake in America
meaning a decent place to live in
meaning a fair wage

and the rest of it.
I say
that is absolute bunk.
I say
we can't afford not to give this guy
named Bashinsky or Tomburello or Schmidt or maybe Murphy
a stake
if we are going to keep Hitler
or somebody worse
out of our country.
I say
our banks are lousy with idle money
we have most of the gold in the world
buried in Kentucky
and if there is a limit
on the food we can raise
on the houses we can build
on the clothes we can make
on the things of every kind that we can produce
we are so far from approaching it
we don't even need to think about it.

Remember what the economists
and all the other -ists
were telling us about Hitler?
How he would go busted in a few months?
How he could never buck the money power
of Britain and France?
How he was just a clown
and could never make the grade?
That ought to teach us
not to pay a particle of attention to the -ists
but to use our eyes
to use our heads.

Americans, you have got to forget all this abracadabra
about what we can afford and can't afford.
When half the shoe factories are shut down
and you need shoes
that doesn't add up.
When half the carpenters are out of jobs
and you're living in a hog-pen
that doesn't add up either.

When the farmers are burning wheat in their furnaces
or getting paychecks from the government
for not raising it
that not only doesn't add up
that's a crime against the people.

Americans
let's think about this Negro problem a little bit.
I don't know what you happen to think about Negroes
but I was raised with them
and I know them
and I am of the opinion
that they are human beings.
I damn well know
they think they are human beings
and expect to be treated as such
and if America doesn't treat them as such
in Florida as well as New York
in Mississippi as well as Ohio
they are going to listen to Hitler
or anybody else
who promises them
justice.

Of course Hitler
wouldn't give them justice
but they don't know that.
America hasn't bothered to educate them about Hitler
but America hasn't bothered to educate them about America either
and since they haven't had much education
they have had to use their eyes
and use their heads
and they have got the idea
that America doesn't mean them
that when we say *all men*
have certain inalienable rights
we don't mean they have
and when we say
all men were created equal
we mean white men.

Now about Latin America.
We have decided to enforce the Monroe Doctrine

and bat the ears off
any European power
that tries to lay hands on any territory in this hemisphere.
Now that is just fine
but let's get straight about a few things.
At the moment
we are lending money to Brazil
which is the main country down there
and where they have the most German colonists
but this money
is going into the hands of a guy named Vargas
who is an absolute dictator
and it wasn't so long ago
that he was having the workers of Brazil
shot down
but he called them all Communists
so that made it OK.

This dictator Vargas
that the American democracy
is supporting this week
because he says he is against Hitler
could easily build himself up
with our money
our public money that belongs to the American people
and next week
go over to Hitler.
What's going to stop him?
Certainly not the Brazilian people
because the Brazilian people
haven't got any say.
Suppose Hitler offers Vargas
a higher price than we do?
Today we buy him.
What's going to keep him bought?
You saw what happened to the French
and what happened to the British
when they tried to buy Hitler and Mussolini.

I say
this business of buying dictators
has to stop
if only because

they won't stay bought.
We have got to be smart for a change.
We have got to go to work with everything we have
in the way of money
influence
political leadership and what not
to establish truly democratic government in the western hemisphere
the only kind of government
nobody can buy.

This means
we must get over to Latin Americans
that the Standard Oil is not us in Venezuela
the nitrate monopoly is not us in Chile
and big American landowners are not us in Mexico.
We
want them to work their problems out in their own way
and if that means
putting the bee on Standard Oil or the nitrate monopoly or the big
    American landowners
that is OK by us
only
they have got to let the people rule
FOR NOBODY
CAN BUY
THE PEOPLE.

IV

POEMS
1941–1944

NEWS ITEM

I see in the paper this morning
where a guy in Gadsden Alabama
by the name of John House
who was organizing rubber workers in a lawful union
against the wishes of the Goodyear Rubber Company and the
    Sheriff of Etowah County
was given a blood transfusion
after being beaten with blackjacks
by five parties unknown.
The Police Chief is "investigating"
and I have a pretty good idea of what that will amount to.
A few years ago they took Sherman Dalrymple
President of the United Rubber Workers of America
out of a peaceable union meeting in Gadsden
and right in front of the Etowah County court house
before the eyes of hundreds including the Sheriff
the deputies
beat him almost to death.
Plenty more
who have tried to organize workers in Etowah County
have had the same thing happen to them.

The Government of the United States
should know about John House
but maybe they won't notice the little item
on the back pages of the Birmingham paper
because the front pages are all filled up with Hitler
and how he is threatening democracy
so I am asking
the Government of the United States
to pay a little attention to this.
To defend democracy
the Government of the United States
is building a lot of munitions plants around the country
with the people's money
because the people want democracy defended
One of these plants is being built at Gadsden

in Etowah County Alabama—
twenty-four million dollars worth of plant to be exact—
twenty-four million dollars of the people's money
going into a county
which isn't even a part of the United States
Or is it?

I think it would be a good idea
for the Government of the United States
to look into this
and see if they can't persuade Etowah
to come back in the Union
If persuasion won't work they might try a little coercion
because the laws of the United States ought to be made good
and as luck would have it
there's a great big army camp at Anniston
just thirty miles away
Not long ago I drove through this camp
and I saw new barracks and tents all over the scenery
and thousands upon thousands of soldiers
getting ready to defend democracy
They looked to me
as if they could do it
and they looked to me
as if they wanted a try at it
Maybe they could get a little practice over in Etowah
before they pitch into
the foreign fascists

THE FACE YOU HAVE SEEN

April has come
April of 1941
the month we were waiting for
through the dark winter
begins . . .

The old man with the face you have seen
tough and kind and none too bright
but lasting
the face you have seen getting on the streetcar
at the mill gate stop
or the gusty corner
now under the blood-soaked handkerchief
looks out at you
with blood oozing down the forehead
from under the handkerchief
and blood on the collar of the old overcoat . . .

"We'll be in it by April"
they said.
Sure enough
the fighting has started
and this old man with the face you have seen
is the first to get hurt.

"Whose America?" somebody asked
and is this the answer?
Another old man
with a face you also have seen
a face you have seen getting out of limousines
at the bank entrance
or the War Department
asks us to remember '94
when the army broke the Pullman strike.
That was a time to forget
I thought
and I think
right now is the worst of all possible times
to ask us to remember . . .

It is April now
the month we were waiting for
but was it for this
that we waited—
the berserk cop with the brandished club
the armored bus spraying gas on the pickets
the mobbing howl of the press
and the rabies in Congress—
"to the electric chair with the strikers"?

Whose America anyhow?
Now in this April
we need to find out.
Yes, all of us need to know whose America
because if it really isn't the America of the old man
with the face which is our face
tough and kind and none too bright
but lasting—
then, well
we are going to have to do some thinking
some mighty hard thinking . . .

This is the April we were waiting for.
This is the April.
This April.
Now.

FREEDOM THE WORD

May 30, 1941
and we are still waiting
waiting for the answer.

What I mean by the answer
is not just something that satisfies your mind
so you stop thinking about the problem
and feel comfortable again
but I mean an answer
that takes hold of you
that won't leave you alone
that makes you act its way
that won't let you act any other way
that you go to sleep with
and wake up with
and it hasn't changed.

John Brown
found that kind of an answer long ago
old John Brown
who took up arms
to free the slaves
and when he was captured and sentenced to hang
the answer didn't change on him
it stayed the same
and when the slaveholders told him to prepare himself for eternity
he told them he was OK thank you
and they were the ones had better start preparing.
The only thing that bothered John Brown
while he was waiting for the slaveholders to hang him
was that his friends up north might try to rescue him from jail
because the answer said
he had to hang.

Freedom:
that was it
that was the answer
but when the big fighting started
not many knew it
they were still mixed up
even Lincoln wasn't sure
thinking it was all about states' rights
the sanctity of the union
and such
not really putting their backs into the job
thinking maybe
it could all be patched up pretty quick
and America could go on
half slave and half free.

We settled that.

Freedom
the word freedom
freedom the word
a good word freedom
but who using it means it?

Freedom for the Poles?
or for the colonels again and the landlords

the jewbaiters who taught Hitler his tricks
and refuged in London at the end of the trail
from Warsaw to Bucharest to Paris
still whet their knives for the Jews
"who betrayed us and brought in the Nazis"?
That's what they're saying.
Is it up to us
to put these Humpty-Dumpties together again?

The fight for freedom
has got to be against Hitler
sure
but for means *for*—
don't forget.

What we've got now
is a half of the answer
and where an answer's concerned
a half's worse than none.
Freedom.
Fight against Hitler.
Fight for?
Fight for freedom meaning really freedom
honest to God meaning freedom?
I have seen men fighting for their freedom
here in America these last months
fighting to make the law mean
what the law says
and the Bill of Rights mean
what the Bill of Rights says.

They won.
It was a hard fight but they won.
The workers of America won the right to organize
even to organize Bethlehem and Ford
but oh the friends of "freedom"
who fought them tooth and toenail . . .

These are the things we can't help remembering
these are the things that give us pause
the beaten picket at the mill gate the tear gas and the riot squad
the kneeling children in the berry fields
the slum

the slums
the slums upon slums upon slums upon slums
and nothing really done
(freedom here? what freedom? whose freedom? when freedom?)
the freedom of children to kneel in the berry fields
(in the image of God)
and the freedom of the tractor to plough under the sharecropper
is not the freedom
we mean to fight for . . .

Writing this
is John Beecher an American of the twelfth generation
which gives me just as good a right to say what I think
as you have Sam Culotta and you Moe Yarmolinsky
who took out your first papers last Tuesday.
I do not have the answer any more than you.
You do not hunger for the answer any more than I.

The answer . . .
Freedom the word
the word freedom
worn smooth in the mouths of the orators
slick as an old coin in the pocket
a word of clean silver though
American silver.
Freedom meaning?
Of the press to fight against freedom in the here and now?
Who put the heat on Bethlehem?
Who put the heat on Ford?
Freedom begins at home.
(The great heart of the press bleeds for the Poles Danes French
    Greeks and Chinese.)
Freedom meaning?
Of the few to own and the rest to be lucky to work?
The old coin freedom is worn slick and smooth
the inscriptions rubbed off and the eagle dim
but it is clean silver
and can be reminted . . .

HERE I STAND

I

Starting from Alabama
on September 8, 1941
I came North
to find out what was going on
what people were thinking feeling getting ready to do or already
     doing
what I could do
more than I was already doing
which was not enough
not nearly enough.

The sun went down on Georgia
behind the silver speeding train.
The red eroded land
went black.
Only the black pines
and the gleam of kerosene in cabin windows
went by.

All through the night waking up
and the same South still
the black and jagged land
plow-wrecked, cashcrop-gutted, rained down to the sea
and the pines
like what's left of an army
straggling home from defeat.

This America
this part of America
this much of America
and what have we done with it?
what are we doing with it?
so the doing is bigger than the talk about doing?
this American South?

Here the last eight years of my life
have gone
working with people in lost unthought-of places
and what to show?

Eight years given up
the years that count
that fix the lines of a man
beyond any future unshaping
except he be hammered to pieces.

Aimed years these were
not years at random
sniffing tonguing this and that
but years like great shells hurled at their objective
or bombs dropped after sighting
years of my full strength
being fully used
and my strength grew the more it was called on.

I learned
that strength is a matter of the made-up mind
the knowing what is to be done
clenched with the will to do it
and the way then comes of itself
obstacles explode into rubble
enemies fall back.

This knowledge then to show
for eight years of going up against
what must be gone against everywhere
if we mean the words we are saying
and no armistice anywhere
least of all in Wilmington, Birmingham, Natchez and Belle Glade
places I know.

How shake off the sense of all this land?
not the South only
but all of it
from cut-over Maine and the fishermen
cursed by the sea's too great bounty
to fat Wisconsin sicklied over with debt
the Dakotas Oklahoma and Texas
where the dark winds blew people off along with the topsoil
and the tractors every year advance
pitiless as tanks
driving more people before them

out to Arizona and California
and the human tides flowing along the valleys
from Agua Fria Yuma Calipatria and Indio
following the cotton the lettuce and the peas
on up the San Joaquin to the Sacramento
and doubling back
all places I have been
things and people I have seen
how shake off the thought of them
or of hideous Baltimore and Philadelphia
street after hideous street
Youngstown Ohio where the mill smoke dirties the snow before it
    even hits the ground
bleak Butte Montana on its nude and tawny hills
poisoned with copper
or Paterson New Jersey?
Silken things shimmer behind Fifth Avenue's acres of plate glass a
    few miles away
but there is no shimmer to Paterson
the silk mills boarded up
the empty streets
the corner loafers
the ugly words chalked on the vacant walls
the smell of stale sweat
(it will not out)
and the grimy quiet.

Aware of this in blood and bone
going to sleep with it
waking up with it
how change
how shake off the sense
of what there is to do
in the here
in the now?
not in any tomorrow
not across distant seas
so easy to promise
mongering words
but mark you
the stink of the lie sticks to the unfelt word
the slick restatement of what proved itself empty

once
and will again.

This is the ax
at the root of faith
this the sharp edge of disbelief.

II
Pulling out of Alexandria
and the drunk in the washroom
lurching and weaving between the shiny bowls
trying to get something off his mind.
He bossed 150 men on a defense job
powder plant arsenal or dam
he didn't make it clear
but what he didn't like
he was sure of.

The blueprints
they made it go round and round
when it ought to go straight
the thing was to get this thing built
not some guy show how smart he was
and the government ought to know about this
no sense to it
no sense at all in going all around a thing
instead of straight through
and he was going to tell the government about it.

"Kill 'em
just kill about twelve of them Germans
the right twelve
and it'd be all over.
You oughtn't to go against
the working sort of people
no time
nowhere."

The silver train on the Potomac bridge
and the city ahead
the dome the shaft the shining sunlit blocks
and the drunk straddled at the window

"Washntn" he reverently says
"Thass my town
Washntn D. C."

    III
Along the stately tedious corridors
in anterooms to air-conditioned offices
(the administrator will see you in a few minutes)
the rugs so soft after sidewalk and tile
sinking down upon soothing and pliable leather
creamy the walls with a slum scene in pastel
and a leader's picture
inscribed
there the obsession returns
the strength-killing word
DECEMBER
over and over again going round
like a victrola record caught in one groove
DECEMBER DECEMBER DECEMBER
what day is today?
a day in December
and tomorrow?
another day in December.
(But it's really September
October comes next and then all of November.)
But that was August, August last year
and coming back to my hotel from being out with people
he stepped from the shadows and touched my arm.
"You remember me?"
Small, stooping, Jewish,
thick glasses making his big eyes bigger
red hair like the outside sign of a deep inward smolder.
Ten years it had been
he then a student in college
I an instructor
and here he was
appearing out of the sultry night of a Washington August
the man with a month for a name
the month when the last leaves fall
in the sleety wind
and the limbs branch black
against the gray sky.

We sat on a bench in the little square facing my hotel
and he said
"You have influence
you know people
maybe you can help me."
"I hope so" I told him calling him by the month which was also
his name.
"I've written a book" he said "the only book that's been written
on the topic" and he told me about it.
"We need a book on that" I said. "There hasn't been a book on it
and there ought to be."
"But I can't get it published" he said. "They tell me it wouldn't
make money. If I can get $500 from some foundation they'll
publish it. I thought maybe you could help me. You know so
many people."
"Yes" I said "I know a great many people. But I have a book too
which I can't get anybody to publish because they think it
wouldn't sell. Not now. Not while everybody is interested in
something else and wanting to forget about our problems here
at home. I can't help myself, so I don't see how there's much
chance of my helping you."
"But I put so much into it" he said.
"And so did I into mine" I said.
"I have a little job here and my wife has" he said "relief jobs
and all the time off the job I put on my book
nights and Saturday afternoons and Sundays
two years steady
and now I can't get it published because it wouldn't make money."
"Yes" I said "that's the way it seems to be."

IV
My friend's voice was warm over the telephone
full of friendship
not to be doubted
"John" he said
"of course we can use you and we will use you if you say so."
"I am saying so" I said "I want to be used
I need to be used
please use me where I can be used."
"John" he said "we can only use 60 per cent of you in the govern-
ment
and you want to give 120

you always have given us that
suppose we put you to work
in five or six months you won't be satisfied
you won't be able to stand the limitations
what you need is a really big job
nothing less will hold you."
"Stop buttering me up" I said.
"I mean it" he said. "You're too creative for the government."

And so, after ten days of going from office to office
I get the truth.
Not wanted.
Oh, in a last extremity, my money all gone, needing to eat, yes,
but my need
not theirs
not my country's.

It is something to get this stated
something to get it in words
worth all the days
of not coming to grips
of sensing the friendship
but sensing also something else
(go somewhere else with your gab and your loitering
Mr. Whitman
and your great concerns
for you make us uncomfortable
and we must get on with our small ones.)

Oh, admitting the importance of detail
and nobody ever paid more attention to detail than I
still there must be something else
and to think that at this time of times
that something else is feared
(the administrator will see you in a few minutes.)

Who I am
is neither here nor there
but that the words could be said . . .
"too creative"
meaning
too full of the seed from which new things grow.

Seed.
The new thing springing.
Though young
I have four children
and I was not uninstructed.
That was all part of it
and I couldn't be careful
or if careful beforehand
the rage of the blood
the unstoppable thing
burst through the dam
in spring flood.

The earth
the wonderful womanly earth
and how can the rain withhold itself
or the seed not plunge
deep into sheath?

I was not prudent.
Prudent in nothing
and when the bridge was before me
the stanchions rising into fog
I took it
across the far below water.

Unthinkable, what we were about to do
but I did not think
(for how can the rain withhold itself
or the seed not plunge?)
and we came to the very ends of the earth
the uttermost point
where the sea beat under
and stairs went down from the lonely beacon
(Drake touched here in the long ago
and we, it seemed, were the next.)
All night around the cabin
the vast Pacific pines dripped on the earth.

May it was
May the next
and the kissed earth quivered

blood beading the white
(who could understand
so right and so wrong?)

White of blossoms of marble and of linen waiting
the dark and pillowed hair
the furious compact
sealed in blood.

(Would that the prow of the Argonauts
had never passed between the dark and moving-together rocks
toward the land of the golden fleece
nor in the forests of Pelion had ever the pines been felled
to make the oars)

V

Three minutes to catch the five o'clock for New York
and there at the ticket window
he stands in line before me
the man with a month for a name
and somehow I am not surprised
nor am I surprised that we are going the same way by the same
    train.

When we are seated and the dome the shaft the shining sunlit
    blocks fly backwards
so soft the power in the stored wires
the streets yards roundhouses Maryland hills and fields do the
    moving
while the train is cradled still.

"Has your book been published?" I ask him.
"No. Has yours?"
"No."

He has lost his job in Washington, a relief job that played out and
    though hundreds are being hired every day he somehow cannot
    be used any more
and his wife has lost her job also for belonging to something she
    had a right to belong to according to the precious charter of
    American liberties but in order to defend these the better the
    authorities are finding it expedient to abridge them in certain
    instances.

Nevertheless in every instance life must go on.
Skating rinks, these days, by contrast to treatises on domestic social
    questions, make money, despite the preoccupation of the popu-
    lace with foreign affairs.
The possibilities of establishing a new skating rink in Baltimore,
    he has been told, are good
and he is on his way there to investigate them unless, perchance, I
    can suggest a better idea
which I at the moment
cannot.

Baltimore flies backward
the red identical rows of houses with white identical steps to the
    sidewalk
the aircraft plant raw and stupendous
with 150 bombers for lack of propellers
ranged helpless on the field
(give pots and pans for propellers)
and no skating rink in evidence.

Next stop
30th Street
(the 30th day)
Philadelphia
(of December)
december december december december
the dark land flying backwards
then lit streets flicking
great shipyard cranes rising into darkness
glimpse of plastic firehearted metal under enormous forging
    hammer
furnace pallor neon sheen and the rails speeding backward along-
    side and silver
the trucks on the joints insisting december december . . .

    VI
The black girl on the bare wall
looks down
a trophy she and a talisman
sole spoils from a lost battle
lips nose thick and the kinky hair braided
but from behind this adventitious mask
all women look out

and you who saw behind the mask and drew the essence
drawing yourself in doing so
and all dear women
the love
the woman being loved and loving
each time and each one always the first one and the first time
(ever virgin)

outside my ninth floor cell
the lights climb up and up
the el streaks like a strict and luminous ruler athwart
the monstrous high-piled blocks

next morning Sunday
and the free air moves in the uninfested glittering unbelievable
       avenue
on into the park
where side by side
hyena and puma are caged
the loping cringe of the one incessant and stricken
somewhere a lion roars and terror shakes the carrion beast
the downslanted hindquarters cower lower
the black and scalded privates quivering contract
then having dunged
the thing resumes his lope
but the puma
unshakably seated
the head high the furred neck and shoulders superb
the marvelous muscles in repose
the eyes green-gray and straight to the front
looking through cages through people through monstrous high-
       piled blocks
and from time to time
the lifted lips
the white-fanged hiss
bespeaking the will never to feed
upon the lion's leavings
nor to pick the bones of the carcass
left behind by the sated wolf.

       VII
"They've turned art into a whorehouse" he said
"not a real whorehouse but a pseudo whorehouse

if it were a real one that would be different
that would be all right.
But here in America
they buy and sell the artist
and then don't use him."

The old man on the couch was speaking
speaking not exactly to me but through me
the furious and undaunted eyes like the eyes of the puma
though dark and plumbless.
"Your friend who drew the head of this black girl
is an artist
you say she works at her art and will not give up
(she will be successful)
but when success comes
do you think she can stand it?
I have seen so many young people
with the gift of seeing and the fidelity to put down what they saw
    just as they saw it
and then they succeed
and that is the end of them."

"I think she will be able to stand it" I said.

"You never know" he said. "The pressure is terrible. America cor-
    rupts her best and puts them to no use. A few stand out
    against it. Only a few."

The puma does not range his cage but sits
and in his sitting is more life compact
than in the hyena's ceaseless circling.
The puma sits not having space to spring.

Hair sprouts from the old man's ears like tasseled corn in sunlight
in May sunlight
but in the newspaper office
(tall temple of liberty, multistoried fane)
December closes back
with the close-lipped man
moulder of popular opinion
who reads the letter presenting me
and then says
"I can think of nothing."

But I am thinking of something
I am thinking how this close-lipped man
having as much as any other perhaps
created a certain climate of opinion
a certain popular skepticism about slogans and crusades
has now reversed himself and must likewise reverse the public mind.
He does not seem to me a happy man
or a man conscious of any presence but his own, and that un-
    welcome.

Was I wrong then, he must be thinking,
(through my fault through my fault through my most grievous
    fault) and am I right now?
Or am I wrong now (the pressure is terrible) though right then and
    what will be the judgment upon me?
Or right both then and now? (The circumstances are entirely dif-
    ferent.)
Or both times wrong? (Things are always mixed. Every slogan is
    partly true and partly false. Every crusade is partly a high em-
    prise and partly a piratical expedition.)

Why do I feel compassion for this successful man
who quite obviously feels none for me
though my formed and confident powers should rot in disuse?

Go away please and leave me alone with my two selves
he would be thinking if his thinking were entirely honest
or with my one half-self whichever it is
for the two must be made one
or the half whole
and there is no time to be lost

circling his cage

    VIII
You could join the Canadian army
I say to myself
and while the ravens provide for your wife and children
shoot craps on a blanket for ha'pennies

    IX
We dance upon the striped hide of a zebra
while the phonograph plays "Tuxedo Junction"

and I tell her about how I was shot at in Tuxedo Junction at twelve
     years of age
the other boy not liking the looks of me and coveting my new
     bicycle.
Twice his 22 cracked but both times he missed me.
Again once while still a boy I was the object of target practice
through being mistaken for a Negro in the dark.
Four times the man shot and four times I heard the heavy calibre
     slugs
spat in the grass of the terrace I scrouged up to.

Time moves on to Mozart and we sit
while in the next room the voice of the man who was born to be a
     bishop
excathedrates with a corpulent catch at the close of each breath.
He categorically hopes (if that be possible) the lousy Russians and
     Germans kill one another off
tens of millions of lives being but a just price to pay
for submitting to bad leadership.
(For lo I have lifted my hand against the working sort of people.)

The plainclothes bishop taking himself canonically off to bed upon
     the stroke of twelve
for he must prepare copy betimes in the morning
having a deadline to meet
and millions wait upon his words
indeed a whole hemisphere
for thousands at his bidding speed
and post o'er land and ocean
waiting diesels throb and the vast motors of planes warm for the
     spuming take-off from blue Biscayne
and so he and his Jehovah to bed
but I linger
for she I sense
has something to say to me.

"I am a happy person
and I have been happy ever since one time in Shanghai
God spoke to me
God really did
and He told me everything was going to be all right
that in fact it was always all right
and He would never leave my side.

"In thirteen months
in a year from October
I shall go back to South Africa
if Hitler is not there before me
and I don't think he will be
do you?"

"No."

"I don't know why I should want to get away from New York
I make more money than I know what to do with
I have this lovely apartment
friends
everything I used to believe I wanted
but I keep thinking about South Africa."

"But why South Africa?"

"It's so free" this woman from Kansas tells me. "It's the freest place
in the world."

        X
Across the screen the stiff and puppet people go
Sovkino's heroic proletarian as like to life as Hercules to me.
"Vodka vodka I must have vodka"
shouts the stagy bearded father
and breaks a strike to get it
while the fiendish bossmen gloat in their mustachios
to see the workers' blood

a short follows
exhibiting the earthly relics and mementos of one P. Chaikovsky
"the ingenious P. Chaikovsky"
a composer of pre-revolutionary times but still a Russian.
We see the P. Chaikovsky museum
his wooden villa mid-Muscovite-Victorian
within doors the bust of P. Chaikovsky
(one almost smells the bayrum on the lifelike whiskers)
the creaking superfluous furniture
the crinkled, yellowed scores on the piano
and capping all
the silk hat with elegant gloves of P. Chaikovsky

and is that all that stays?

suddenly through the door they come
a troop of people
no proletarian heroes these nor vodka-shouters
but real
their imperfections writ large upon them
their yearnings also—
the heavy peasant forehead and the lips agape
(here dwelt the ingenious P. Chaikovsky, sainted man of music)
struggling to absorb the mystic influence from the holy ikons
silk hat with elegant gloves crinkled yellowed scores and bust
wanting the thing that is not here

the others
a boy in gunboat shoes scuffling and abashed
(like my boy David)
a clodlike girl with litten eyes
two shavenheaded men in Red Army blouses and starred caps in
     knotted hands
then all at once the music of the Pathétique
the ageless pain
bursting from the sound-track
existing from and by itself
shoulderblades crawl and needles penetrate the spine
the woe

ye who are about to die
or live far worse than dying
peasant forehead with your lips agape
scuffling boy like my boy David
girl with litten eyes
Red Army men
I salute you

wild with all regret the music and within me

I salute you
race humaine

   XI
ever virgin
she is coming toward me
across vast breadth of earth
night of stars above and stars under

stars unmoving and changeless above
stars under single or clustered or nebulae
hued cuprous bloodred whiteblue of ladled steel green like first
　　shoots pricking erect from the soil in spring

a whole arc of the world swinging under
tiny winking star by itself where the farmer rouses himself and
　　lighting his smoky lamp commences his long day
cuprous sun where the jook-joint stays open all night
the soldier and the coal-heaver start for each other with beer
　　bottles
the bouncer goes to work with his blackjack
and the unmilked slut pukes all over the table

twin beams on the highway delicate gemini
cross-country truck thunderous and huge
at the wheel the man awake aware
muscled controlled master of tons powered with wheels
or backseat lovers returning
all glandular tension relieved
the commemorative handkerchief dropped by the roadside
and the consummation by finger

constellation of a town
blue-windowed mill where spindles twirl
and weary women watch
pushing back their raveling hair from hungry hatchet faces
gas-stations lunch-wagons and the vacant main street beaded
the felt legion of the tired sleeping
the dome the shaft the shrouded unlit blocks
tilted up to window and circling slow and nearer
sad Lincoln watching and the pool reflecting

the hushed remote descent and muffled stop

(she does not live here . . . caged in this below . . where minutes
　　tick)

roaring it eats the field
earthfast planes hangars trees go storming by
now tail up and triumphantly thundering
until soft upon air it rests
and freely mounts
the earth swinging easily under

over white waves and rolling breakers of fog
the sun gleaming on them
and on wings of riveted silver
quivering in the rush of unseen air
she is coming toward me
ever virgin

the city is washed in fog
great buildings push up
tops lost in the moist
the morning Sunday-still
still almost as woods as vast Pacific pines
dripping on the earth

(and how can the rain withhold itself
or the seed not plunge?)

it is sixteen years since the whippoorwill sang in the pines
"Moonwinx" the place is called now with cabins and beer and a
      nickelodeon outblaring the whippoorwill
but one must never return to a once hallowed ground
never go back to recapture
going onward always

ever virgin
ever new
birth-pangs you have known four times through me
and yet
the wonder
insatiable the need

for sixteen years I have explored this precious land
its lovely hills and valleys
gentle moulded vistas
dark woods and streams
and still when I debark upon its shore
coming home from Colchis
as fresh it is as sweet as fragrant with all right smells of earth
as sixteen years ago when first I planted standard here

ever virgin

you wept
when the milk would not come the last time

and your tears were hot as nitric acid
spilled over me once and my shoes shrivelled my socks plucked off
    in flakes
and on my eaten flesh the bare and branching veins were plain as
    winter trees against the sky.
Those scars I carry yet but the acid of your tears burnt deeper

forgive

through my most grievous fault

          but, by all above,
these blenches gave my heart another youth

home
the always unknown place
that must be known in whole and part
so known that no small bit escapes or ever shall
known to thinking seeing touching hearing smelling tasting brain
through eyes lips tongue teeth nose ears fingers toes and every end
    of nerve in skin that gladly would be flayed
to know the closer

    XII
Coming four flights down from the borrowed room the fog has
    lifted
and the block lies quiet in the sunshine
next door there is a tree
imagine
a tree shadowing the pavement
and under it
as under his own vine and figtree
sits the owner of the property
FURNISHED ROOMS
and bright blue paint on doors on window frames
with view of tree

we advance and ask

"nah" he smirking says
"no room for you"
(for such as you implied)

"you aren't imagining things?" I question

"nah nah"

"then where can we find a room?"
(with blue on door and window frames implied and view of tree)

he didn't know he couldn't say in all New York
not there
most positively not
nah nah

and then the mirth of it
the wonderful and unintended compliment
comes home
and arms on curve of other's hip we go
laughing up the sunlit street
to think
that after sixteen years
fifteen in lawful wedlock
with christened children four
we can be taken for adulterers
so happy we so suspect to the public eye

   XIII
after the grim dark tunneling grind
at 125th the three get on
glowing from the sun
collars open armpits ringed with wet
two have poking sheaves of fishpoles
one a basket
the Irishman just right
poised on the perilous crest
(another drink would send him spiraling down)
the torpid subway car awakes
Irishman adjusts his poles with antic care
once, he says, he poked them in a fan
and hell to pay
with dust and stuff all over everybody

the gray-haired spinster next him at the window
turns a face no longer gray and pinched
but full of love, a lovely face, upon him
and down the aisle a little boy leans out to see and hear

unspoken the question of all the car
all the car wondering

what did you guys catch
out in the sun on the cool salt water
and heard old Triton blow his wreathed horn?

he of the basket senses the question
and with all simulated pomp
with mock and priestly ceremony
opens wide the lid of wicker
drawing forth a crab
a huge and well-clawed crab
and waves him in the aisle
but the poor dead crab
does not respond
the limp dead flippers dangle
and the claws hang listless down

this crab died that we might live
peace be unto his fierce and tameless soul
could a crab wish peace
but the sight of him there
the armored corpse
ivory mottling into red
sends salt and sunwashed air through all the car

XIV

Pell-mell rushing down the steps
hold the door back and we are on
the subway starts the columns flicker past
and the smooth dark tunnel flows along

uptown though not down
as we meant to go
so off at the next station up to the street across and down into the
    fetid glow
the wait long and (pardon me, madam, I wish to make a purchase)
    nothing to do but read the advertisements
then back to Grand Central

the sign not seen until doors closed behind us and the local resum-
    ing its grind
EXPRESS TRAINS NOT RUNNING
alone then under the tireless lights

except for the drunk asleep on the steps
(prickle at the base of the brain
are you a man?
now it will be seen)

Slowly the cast assembles
first a slender youth with curly hair
schooled to law and order he awakens the drunk on the steps
it is not permitted he softly warns
and the drunk erupts into noise
then lights a cigarette
which likewise is not permitted
but the slender youth with curly hair
edges discreetly away

two couples appear
making with us
three couples
all minding our own business

the drunk staggers to his feet

plan of campaign:
a right to the jaw
and left to the sodden belly
should he still show fight
160 pounds at him from ten paces
knee to the groin
then thumbs in the eyepits
hammering skull on concrete

his first quarry couple number one
he approaches them and they flush to the next bay
whereupon he deploys against couple number two
the male leads the retreat
looking unmanned
his female some paces behind
our turn now
and the drunk starts over

halfway I meet him
and he wavers to a stop

campaign plan or no
you can't hit such a thing

stiff-armed at the junction of neck and chin
with all power and no warning he topples backward
then quietly and without a word of remonstrance
goes away with recovered equilibrium

under the tireless lights the mute cast watches
until the appeaser
the slender youth with curly hair
takes charge
rushing to soothe the aggressor

soon querulous words are heard
"I wasn't doing a thing to him"
"He just came up and knocked the hell out of me"
"He wanted to kill me"
then the drunk to me
"You're tough, aren't you?"
"Where you're concerned" I say "yes I'm tough."
"When that subway train comes" he says from over in his bay in
        the arms of the appeaser
"and we get on, I'm going to punch you right in the nose."
"Punch here, where the punching is good" I suggest and come over,
        sick at heart, but ready.
No answering move or word from his corner
I return to my wife and take from her
the papers I gave her to hold

again it begins
the wounded words
"I wasn't doing a thing to him"
and the appeaser comes over to us
"You better move on" he says
"he's drunk and you can't do anything with him
he'll heckle you as long as you stand here."

"Let him heckle" I say "but he'd better do his heckling from
where he is."

"If I were you" the appeaser says "I'd move on."
"I'm not moving" I say.

The mute cast watches under the tireless lights
and the train coming we board it at the exact point where we've
    been waiting
except for the drunk
who gets on the car ahead

back in the room I wash and wash
the hand that touched him

    XV
Through the warm days
brightened by sun
and the warm nights
suffused by moon
insatiable love seeking solitude
companionship seeking crowds
and both were found in full measure

the lost
if lost
refound and more

he of the black palm
the once powerful
now all lips and lungs
roaring in bars
shhh from all sides shhh he hears
"I don't know whether you are brother and sister"
he said—"God love ye—
or husband and wife."

"We've been married a long time" we told him.

"Then get on the Third Avenue El" he told us.
"I can take you places they'd kill you for a nickel
this town is corrupt
but me I'm a human being
I like to see things growing
things pushing up
get on the Third Avenue El
and go out to the park
56 blocks of it

look at the swans
and you'll get married all over again"

waving his huge and flabby arms
huge from digging anthracite in Shamokin Pennsylvania
flabby from lifting glasses in New York bars
("Ale" he said roaring "don't give me any of your beer")
he staggers across Fourteenth Street
stopping traffic with his black imperative palm
God love him

    so quickly they go
    the days and nights of warmth

    this thought is as a death, which cannot choose
    but weep to have that which it fears to lose

    and again alone

MAN NOT WANTED

    men who can do what is wanted done
    in this town
    are a dime a dozen
    on a falling market
    sell yourself sell yourself sell yourself

    and be not used

    Here I stand
    John Beecher on the block
    sound of wind and limb and fully formed
    fit to bear the burden of my time
    until my spine cracks under the weight

    Do I hear any bids?

October, 1941

WE WANT MORE SAY

It was dark
coming into Pittsburgh
and the night was misty too
but all up and down the river valleys
the mills were full of light
cranes raising ingots from the glowing pits
blooms slabs billets bars and shapes streaking hot through the
    rolls
whitehot seethe from open hearth peepholes
spouts of high fire melting into fume
blast furnace slag flowing golden on the dumps
even beehive ovens
I never thought I'd see coked up again
winking red in smoky wasteful rows . . .
working for defense
all up and down the Allegheny and the Monongahela
the Ohio the Mahoning and the Beaver
the mills the furnaces the powerhouses cokeplants machine shops
    and foundries
working all night for defense.

Next day in Pittsburgh was dark
with wet snow
coming down through the smoke
down the black buildings
making black slush on the sidewalks.
The streetcar took me
out past the J&L mills
across the Monongahela to the Mesta Machine Works
through Homestead where they smashed the union in '92
across the river again to Braddock
and along the Edgar Thomson plant
to the view of great concrete arches bridging the valley
with Westinghouse shops underneath
which everybody has seen in the slick Westinghouse ad
only the ad leaves out the housing
and everybody ought to see that too . . .
When I got back to Pittsburgh
I had gone 20 or 30 miles on the streetcar
and the men who are working for defense

in J&L Steel in Mesta Machine in Carnegie and in Westinghouse
    Electric
got on and off at their stops
going to and from work
and in all those miles
I didn't see one what you might call American home.
I saw plenty of smoke-black shacks perched on the hillsides
and block upon block upon block of packed filthy brick with
    windows and doors in it and apparently people
because plenty of kids were playing in the slushy streets
and on rubbishy lots.
Men kept getting on and off that car
going to work
coming from work
and they all looked glad about it in a quiet way
but nobody had on a silk shirt yet.
The closest to that
was a young guy sporting a greasy cap
plastered with different colored CIO buttons
showing he'd been keeping up his dues since way back
and was damn proud of it.

That night I went to a banquet
for Pittsburgh's "Man of the Year"
and after a lot of speeches about him
the man himself spoke
and it seemed to me as I watched his eyes
and as I listened to his words
that he knew he was talking
not just to the people who came there to honor him
but to all the people in this country
and it seemed to me also
that this man was more than just this man
but all the men back of him
those not knowing it equally with those knowing
those before his time and those of it and those to come after
their thoughts in his mind
their desires in his heart
their words in his mouth . . .
The thing he was saying was
what Americans have always been saying
but America has never caught up with . . .
just that we all of us belong

and nobody belongs any more than anybody else does
and America belongs to all of us.
And if America is in danger
we will defend America
all of us that is will defend all of us
but most of us will not defend
a few of us
which has happened before
nor will most of us
let a few of us
run America for the advantage of a few
which is happening now
even now . . .
the most of us want a say
in how we shall live and how we shall work
in how industry shall be run—
we work there
we have ideas
we could help—
and since we are going to have to do
whatever fighting and dying are necessary
we want more say in defense . . .
we are loyal Americans
and because we are
we want more say . . .
These are my words
but his meaning
and it doesn't matter that his name was Phil Murray
and that he is head of the CIO
because like I say
he wasn't talking just for himself
but for all the men back of him
those not knowing it equally with those knowing
those before his time and those of it and those to come after
their thoughts in his mind
their desires in his heart
their words in his mouth . . .
a few of us had better be listening.

AFTER EIGHTY YEARS

I

Lincoln was pushed into it
they are still telling us
yes
after eighty years
they are still handing us that

I'd put it this way
Lincoln was just slow to catch on
slow to take hold
like many another man
trusting the experts but not himself fully
not really believing
in what he was fighting for
because he hadn't made his own mind up

Once Lincoln made his mind up
and wrote:
"thenceforward and forever free"
he started being the Lincoln we remember
and the war for Union
turned into a people's war
that could not be lost
Emancipation
kept England off the South's side
because the English working people
could not be made to fight for slavery

Emancipation
brought the Negroes in on the North's side
and turned the scale
Lincoln said so then
but after eighty years our school history books
still have nothing to say
about the 200,000 Negro soldiers and sailors
who lost a third of their number
fighting for their freedom and the Union
while the South warned
"none will be taken prisoners"
A Memphis slavedealer turned general
Nathan Bedford Forrest

captured Fort Pillow on the Mississippi
having ten men to the Union's one
and there under the white flags of surrender
bayoneted to death or buried alive
the Negro wounded
penned the Negro prisoners in wooden buildings
then burned them down
It was another story
at Port Hudson, Ship Island, Fort Wagner and Nashville
where Negroes fought on even terms
and it was a far different story
that day in 1865
when black cavalry rode into Richmond
at the head of Grant's army
Behind these black fighters
were black workers for freedom
in hundreds of thousands
on the docks where munitions were unloaded
on Union fortifications from the Red River to the James and
    Potomac
builders teamsters cooks and nurses of the wounded
while by the hundreds of thousands
Negroes left their plows in the fields of slavery
seeking refuge in the camps of the blue armies
seeking work in freed fields
then having found it
they plowed to feed and clothe blue armies
while gray armies
went bare and hungry
After eighty years
we ought to know these things
better than we do

    II
Eighty years
are a long while to be waiting
for somebody to finish
what Lincoln began

Starting in 1863
Negro Americans with their own blood and toil
have bought and paid for freedom
full and unconditional

ten times over
and now in 1943
Negro Americans
in the army and the navy
by the hundreds of thousands
are fighting for the world's freedom
as well as their own . . .

In Lowndes County Alabama
Negroes are more than 85 per cent of all the people
but in all that county
not one Negro votes
not one Negro is called Mister by white people
and the few Negroes who own land
don't dare build themselves decent homes
for fear the white folks would resent it
I saw a tumbledown tenant cabin in Lowndes
from which three dark boys had gone North
two of them are college deans now and the third a scientist

A few years back
the sharecroppers down in Lowndes tried to organize
because somebody from the outside
came in and told them
the President of the United States said they had a right to
They counted the bodies they found afterward
the ones shot on dry land
and the ones that washed up bound hand and foot
on the Alabama River bank
but there were plenty still missing
One planter told me
he'd been merciful himself
he just called a meeting of his croppers
in the church
and publicly whipped
the two or three that got mixed up in the union
that taught the rest of them a lesson
he told me

Between 1935 and 1940
400,000 farms were wiped off the southern map
400,000 families had to pull up stakes
more than 2,000,000 people cut adrift

You've heard about the white farmers
from Oklahoma, Texas and Arkansas
and who went to California
and maybe you saw "The Grapes of Wrath"
but did you know
40,000 families were tractored out in Alabama
mostly Negroes
more people than lost out in Oklahoma?

No
we don't hear about them
nor about the 35,000 families in Georgia
who lost their chance to make a crop
they were mostly Negroes too

Where they all went
nobody exactly knows
some lived on where they were
in their little shacks and cabins
catching what wagehand work there was
sixty cents a day from can till can't
or picking cotton at 75¢ a hundred
some moved to town and went on relief
some hit the migrant trails
from Louisiana up through Arkansas and Kentucky on into
    Michigan
from Florida on up the coast to Lake Ontario and Maine

I got to know these people
down in Florida
and I would like to say something about them

They were living on the canal banks
in stinking quarters and barracks
sometimes thirteen people in a room
or in tarpaper huts and shelters in the weeds
and every morning before dawn came
they climbed on to trucks in the quarters
bound for the beanfields
where all day
everybody that could pick
down to the five and six year olds
picked

kneeling in the black Everglades muck.
It would be dark night again
when they got back to quarters
and all night long
the jook joints stayed open
so whiskey dice and women
could eat up the earnings of the day

That was the white growers' idea
of how to hold labor—
keep the Negroes broke
they said
and instead of a church or a school
a grower would build a jook joint
at the center of his quarters
to get back at night
what he paid out in the day

When the government came in
and started building a model camp for the Negroes
with screened shelters and shower baths and flush toilets
an infirmary a community center a school and playgrounds
laundry tubs and electric irons
the growers raised hell
what was the government's idea anyway
ruining the rental value of their canal bank quarters
and fixing to ruin their labor with a lot of useless luxury
besides the Negroes wouldn't use the camp
they liked to be dirty
they liked to be diseased
they liked to be vicious

When the growers saw
the government was going ahead anyway
they said
"You will have to hire a bunch of camp guards
white men
and have them patrol the camp
with clubs and pistols
or the Negroes
won't pay the rent
they will stop working entirely
and they will take the camp to pieces"

Let me tell you what happened
I know
because I was there
and I was in charge of the camp

When the day came to open
we just opened the gate
and let anybody in that wanted to come in
no hand-picking no references or anything like that
it was enough for us
that a family wanted to live there
and not on the canal bank

We didn't hire any white guards either
and nobody carried a club or a pistol
in all that camp that held a thousand people

We just got them altogether in the community center
and told them it was their camp
and they could make it a bad camp
or they could make it a good camp
that was up to them
and there wouldn't be any laws or ordinances
except the ones they made for themselves
through their elected Council

Then for a week
they had a campaign in camp
with people running for office the first time in their lives
and after the campaign
people voted for the people they wanted to represent them
for the first time in their lives
and after it was over
they celebrated with a big dance in the community center
and nobody got drunk and disorderly
and nobody cut anybody with a knife
and the only reason was
they had themselves a Council . . .
after that
the Council made the laws and ordinances

Council said
nobody's dog could run around loose

he had to be tied up
Council said
a man couldn't beat his wife up in camp
and when a man came in drunk one night and did
he was out of camp by morning
Council said
people had to pay their rent
because out of that rent money
came camp baseball equipment
and it kept up the nursery school
so when people wouldn't pay
Council put them out . . .
finally Council said
it's a long way to any store
we ought to have our own store
and that's how the co-op started
without a dollar in it
the people didn't put up . . .

Some of the men and women on that Council
couldn't so much as write their names
remember these were just country Negroes
off sharecrop farms in Georgia and Alabama
just common ordinary cottonpickers
the kind
Lowndes County planters say
would ruin the country
if they had the vote . . .

All I know is
my eyes have seen
democracy work

        III
Freedom
is a whole lot more
than just not being owned by somebody.
Lincoln knew that

Freedom starts with not being owned
but it also means
having a say in how you are governed

a home you can call yours
land if you're a farmer
that you can stay on year after year
hold it and improve it and get the benefit of it
either working for yourself alone
or a lot of farmers altogether working one big farm
for the good of all
and freedom means if you're a worker
the chance to learn the job of your choice
and the right to work at that job

Now
the United States government is putting up hundreds of millions
        of dollars
to teach new trades to citizens
both men and women
so they can build the planes and tanks the ships and guns
we must have to win
I was down in Georgia
looking over this government training program
and I saw fine new shops
full of the most up-to-date machinery
millions of dollars worth
and I saw where thousands of white people
men and women
were being taught at the expense of the government
how to weld ships and rivet airplanes and the rest
but I didn't see any Negroes in the shops
though Negroes are more than one out of every three
of Georgia's people
so I asked where were they . . .
this was kind of embarrassing to the authorities
they admitted they weren't training many
and said the reason was
the Negroes couldn't get jobs
even if they were trained
so there wasn't any use training them . . .

I had to go a long way in Georgia
to find any Negroes getting training
and when I found them
this is what I saw . . .

bare classrooms with benches and blackboards
not a lathe nor a drill press nor a welding machine in the place
men trying to learn through their eyes
what could only be learned through their hands

In all of Georgia
not one Negro woman
was getting even this kind of training
and when I asked why not
the authorities said to me surprised
"If Negro women could get war jobs
what would people do for cooks?"

Then there were the Negro carpenters
I talked to in Houston, Texas
two hundred of them in Houston
men who had been carpenters all their lives
and the white carpenters wouldn't let them in the union
and that meant they couldn't even work
on the Negro housing project
or on any kind of war building that was going on
and since there wasn't anything else left to work on
they were getting desperate . . .

There was a Negro welding class in Houston
just like the white classes
the whites got jobs welding in the shipyards
the day they finished their course
but the Negro welders
are working at common labor
or at nothing . . .

So it goes
all over the South
in munitions at Memphis
aircraft at Dallas and Nashville
at the Macon arsenal and Pascagoula shipyard
no skilled jobs for Negroes
and in many places
no unskilled ones either . . .
just whatever happens to be left over
when the white people are used up
or whatever work is too hot heavy or nasty

for white people to do
is what the Negroes get . . .
that's the way it still is
after eighty years

IV
"Thenceforward and forever free"
were Lincoln's words
but he didn't stop there
no
he said more:
"and the Executive government of the United States,
including the military and naval authority thereof,
will recognize and maintain the freedom of such persons,
and will do no act or acts to repress such persons,
or any of them, in any efforts they may make for their
actual freedom."

Isn't it about time after eighty years
to make good on this
and to make good on
the Thirteenth Fourteenth and Fifteenth Amendments
to the Constitution of the United States?

I know there's a war on
but what is this war about anyway
how can we believe
how can the world's people believe
we mean to spread the light of freedom to the world's four corners
when there is such darkness
in America's own house?

Soon
it will be too late

JOSIAH TURNBULL TOOK NO PART IN POLITICS

Josiah Turnbull took no part in politics
toasting by the stove there
in his snug Philadelphia parlor
while the blizzard swirled
against the frosted panes
yes he congratulated himself
that he hadn't got mixed up
in anything political
but just attended to his own business

I wish I had lived in ancient Rome
in the days of the Gracchi
Josiah thought closing his Plutarch
ah with what dignity
the noble Romans went to their deaths
for their political beliefs
for liberty and justice
verily
Josiah thought knocking the ashes from his pipe
we have fallen upon evil days
and it behooves a man
to hold aloof
from the brawl in the marketplace
as I have done . . .

The door opened from the street
and a blast of cold
swept in from the hall
bending the lamp flames
Josiah could hear the redcoat Major
stamping the snow from his boots very carefully
before going upstairs to his room
the Major was always so correct
it was no hardship at all
to have him billeted there
and he paid for his lodging in gold

not like these Continentals
mechanics and country louts in stinking rags
with no gold or even silver to their names
but only paper

dirty worthless paper money
"not worth a Continental"
yes whatever the rights and wrongs of it might be
and there was much to be said on both sides
the British were the ones to do business with
and that very day
Josiah had made a most profitable bargain
with the British quartermaster
to deliver meat and grain for the garrison

there was the risk always
that the starving Continentals
encamped at the Valley Forge
might make a foray from their lair
and seize the farmers' wagons on the road
but it was Josiah's policy
to pay the farmers
only upon delivery of their produce in the city
so he did not stand to lose
whatever befell . . .

Josiah Turnbull stretched and yawned deeply
in his snug Philadelphia parlor
comfortably reflecting
that he took no part in politics

WE ARE THE AMERICANS
A Campaign Document: 1944

I am
Joseph H. McIlhenny Ph.D.
who in the year 1932
was fired from my instructorship in psychology
at $1800 a year
the reason given by the university
"unavoidable retrenchments of staff"
the result

my wife's death
and the death of our child inside her
I found her with her head in the oven
and the gas jets on
unlit
I have no more to say
except
that whoever brings back times like those
has me to deal with . . .

I am
Alex Bukowski a seaman
torpedoed twice in this war
but still kicking
and still delivering the goods
I am one of the men
Tom Dewey
Governor of New York
beat out of their votes in this election
knowing that I
and all the other seamen
had his number
We still have
and it's coming up . . .

I am
George Nakomis
melter on the open hearth
with two boys in the Navy
somewhere in the South Pacific
Since Pearl Harbor
I have tapped more heats on my turn
armorplate steel most of it
than any other melter in Homestead Works
and none of it checked "off specifications" either
but Dewey's man Pegler
says I oughtn't to be allowed to vote
because I was born on the other side
What wouldn't I give
to get my hands on those two guys . . .

I am
Virginia Sparks the wife of Wallace Sparks

and mother of his three soldier sons
who saw in Hoover's day
the farm sold out from under him
that he his father and his grandfather
had plowed their lives into
Wallace is a quiet man
a gentle man
a man who supports the church
but I was afraid then
for his immortal soul
when he raved of killing in his sleep . . .

I am
Theordis Jackson, Negro
a GI on the docks in Naples
unloading ships
but before the war
I followed the crops on the East Coast
and I remember how it was
when the New Deal came in and helped us
with camps to live in that were decent
and hospitals for the sick folks
and relief money
that time the frost killed out the crops
and there wasn't anything to pick
I remember how it was before that
in the sugar cane the celery and the beans
a whole family in one stinking room
two cents a bucket for your water
cheating you on your pay
and if you said anything
they'd like as not kill you
and throw your body in the canal
I can't vote
because Congress threw the President's bill out
but after I get back I will by God
and I know what for . . .

I am
a man who once worked at the bench alongside of you
or leaned on the bar with his foot on the same rail
it doesn't much matter who
for you'll never see me again

There I was on the beach running inland with the rest
and feeling a lot better than in the boat
because at last there was something to do
and that was the finish
Whatever hit me
I never felt it
I don't exactly want you to feel sorry for me
and I don't care whether you remember me even
only
I wouldn't like it to happen
for you to forget what brought me to that beach
and where I was headed for . . .

THEIR BLOOD CRIES OUT

I

Loving that part of the wide earth he was born on
though it was white man's country and he black
each year he laid by a few dollars
from his sharecrop half of the cotton
he and his family eating light to do it
going ragged and barefoot even in the wintertime
till he got his own piece of this earth
bought from the county for back taxes
and they wrote his name down as owner
there on the big book in the Court House
at Liberty (meaning freedom)
Amite (meaning friendship) County
Mississippi

The white men who had owned the land
but hadn't paid the taxes
came after him then with bullwhips
to teach him this was white man's country
and when the three of them had worn themselves out
stripping the meat from his back

he was still not dead and they figured he might talk
so they cut his tongue out with a switchblade

He died
and his blood soaked into the earth he was born on
the earth he had bought with his toil
and with his children's hunger

II

Loving that reach of the wide sea he was born on
though it was white man's ocean and he black
he sailed it from a boy
fighting the rigging on the old four-masters
heaving coal down below on the freighters
standing watch at the wheel on the icy nights
while the years passed
and when the skipper cursed him for his color
or shipmates wouldn't share his foc'sle for it
he set his teeth and said nothing
but saved every scrap of writing
that proved he'd shipped AB or fireman
and every nickel of his pay
for his folks ashore

One war he sailed through
and they never got him
though he was nine days in a lifeboat
and when the next war came
he was about ready to quit
having the house all paid for
and something put by to live on
but he was needed

It was dusk when the planes struck
and he was at the wheel
he just slumped and that was all
until next day his corpse sewn in canvas
slid out from under the starry flag
into the wide sea he was born on

III

You ask me
what would I do if I were a Negro?

and I keep thinking of these two
who died
one on land and one at sea
murdered

If I were a Negro
I would swear the same oath I am swearing now
to avenge these men
and all the men like them and the women and children
white black yellow and brown
whose blood cries out for vengeance
all over the world

Being a Negro would change nothing
the same men would be my brothers
for brothers are not known by the color of their skins
but by what is in their hearts
backed up by their deeds
and by their lives
when it comes to that

WHITE FOAM BREAKING

Hearing that he is dead
all I can think of
is the white foam breaking
over the spillway
and the lights in the hills

Who are these boys and girls reading by these lights
what lessons are they studying?

After forty years in the Congress of the United States
George Norris died simply a citizen
and in the Senate seat
which he had made more feared by the strong few
more loved by the weak many

than ever a Senate seat before
sat a small-town undertaker
destroying his work like a weevil in the good wheat

Nebraska
thanks for forty years of George Norris
who nourished the spirit of all this land
as your wheat the growing bodies of our children
How you must feel today
Nebraska
we know
who have also struck down blindly
the ones who loved us
and when it was too late
repented

Nebraska your treeless earth
spreads level to the sky's edge
your golden grain upturned to the sun and the blue
it's a long, long way from here
to Tennessee's hills
the rain-blackened cabins in the coves
the thin corn clinging to the slopes
the haggard children
the white water of the rushing streams

What is Tennessee to us?
you said
We want a man who will work for Nebraska
first last and all the time

George Norris grew too big for you
Nebraska
Your great plains bred a vision
vast as themselves and as bountiful

The hills and the plains are one earth
George Norris saw
and the people of both
one nation indivisible

Omaha Lincoln McCook and Grand Forks
the neighbor up the block
or beside the windmill whirling on the far horizon

are Nebraska you said
and when the Sheriff came to seize Jim's farm
you grabbed the pitchfork and went over

But when the people of Prague
of Warsaw Paris Athens Kharkov
wept in the streets as the hobnails rang on their cobbles
George Norris grabbed his pitchfork

Perhaps you understand him better
Nebraska
now that the neighbor up the block
or beside the windmill whirling on the far horizon
has a gold star in his parlor window

I intend to do as much as I can
George Norris said
the old man of 83
with the young heart
You tried to break it Nebraska
but it was too big for you
you were in it
but it had room for all the rest of us besides

He is gone
the simple citizen who marched at the head of us
but the march goes on
We march toward that America
which sleeps in the seeds he planted and others before him
as sure to grow
as wheat on Nebraska plains

He is dead
but the white foam breaks
over the spillway
and the lights in the hills
come on

V

OBSERVE
THE TIME

An Everyday
Tragedy in Verse,
1955

I

"I like my women big," he said
and with his narrowed eyes appraised
her every part as if he were
a butcher and she just livestock
upon the hoof. How dared he? Yet
for once her caustic lips framed no
reproof. She blushed instead. What lurked
within this outcast that could so
compel and paralyze her will?
Beyond his huge and hairy body
surmounted by a tousled graystreaked
mass of uncut hair which matched
the unshorn stubble of his cheeks
and brutal chin she saw the sands
and then the curving scimitar
of surf that flashed against the shore.
The day was clear and blue. The sea
spread glittering far down to where
the coast beyond Carmel dissolved
in misty seacliffs. There the range
came crowding to the water's edge,
sea lions played and sunned themselves
upon the offshore rocks and birds
seized fish caught in the undertow.
And would she too be seized by this
dark cormorant whose prey was woman,
she who had always broken free
and swum unscathed away from each
marauding beak that sought to take her?
The roller coaster by the boardwalk
climbed up its track and paused and then
roared hurtling down the giant dip.
The frightened screams of riders broke
like shattering glass upon the air.
Her shoulders crawled and sudden cold

knifed along her sunwarmed spine.
The males upon the beach were staring.
Six feet of golden female flesh,
all built to perfect scale, drew eyes
and sometimes whistles as she passed.
If once she had resented it
she took it now as only due
and let those greedy glances clutch
at her cool belly's curve in vain
while, as she passed, rich-rounded hips
undulantly scorned them all.
She sat down on the sand and Lew
spread all his tawny length beside her
like some great watchful jungle cat.
"Tell me about yourself," he said,
"Margaret." A murky smile
lit up his face and smouldered out.
"There isn't too much to tell," she said.
"I've always lived in San Francisco.
Parochial school of course and then
Immaculate Conception. Worked
at the Emporium and tried
to take some college courses too.
Then gave it up and got a job
with the phone company. Night shifts
some weeks so Mama got confused.
I could stay out all night in bars
with sailors and she wouldn't know.
Then she caught on but I just told her
that what I did at three AM
I could as easily do at three
PM and she'd just have to trust me."
"Well did she?"
                "No."
                        "And now?"
                                "She still
distrusts me. She and my dear brother."
"It's almost three PM," Lew said.
"Let's go and find us a motel."
"Not now and not at three AM."
"What did you mean about the sailors?"
"Not what you think."
                "I hate a teaser."

"I'm not a teaser."
                "What are you then?"
"I'm still a virgin," she said proudly.
"What's that?" He snickered. "Something good?
Something you can trade for money?"
"Whatever it is," she said, "I plan
to keep it till some man persuades
me otherwise. That won't be you."
"I wouldn't be too sure," he said.
"I kind of specialize in virgins."
That smouldering smile again. It took
the edge off what he said and yet
he wasn't joking. By no means.
A bad hombre this, a psychopath
like those she'd read of in her course
who live to hurt and hurt again.
But why, she asked herself, but why
was she so fascinated by him?
What could his secret be?

                        "I ought
to slap your face," she said, "and if
you keep this up I will, right here
in public."
                "Women make me sick,"
he only said and turned away
his body from her on the sand.
"Why do we make you sick?" she asked.
"Because you're all such phonies."
                        "How?"
"You know how. You kid yourselves.
You don't kid me though. Not a bit.
I sized you up right from the first."
She was amused and pleased to have
so nettled him. Archly she asked,
"How did you size me up?"
                        Lew turned
and faced her, reared upon an elbow.
"For just another teaser out
for kicks. A stop-and-go-gal. The kind
just begging for it till you take
them up. 'Quit, or I'll call the cops!
The green light's changed to red! Throw in
the clutch, step on the brakes!' That's you."

"How can I help it if I'm pure
and mean to stay that way?" she said.
"You're pure all right." He sneered. "Work up
a man until he gets the ache,
or if you're feeling generous
you let him rub himself against you
until you both are satisfied.
But still you're pure as driven snow
as long as nothing gets unzipped.
That's for the birds. Give me some bitch,
some slot machine who spreads her legs
to any man with twenty dollars."
She was too shocked and sick to answer
and yet she thought, "I've asked for this.
For years I've had it coming to me.
Bad as he is, I'm worse than he."

She had exulted in her power.
Back seat and park bench clinches first.
The antagonists she tussled with
in these encounters she had long
forgotten. All who sought her arms
received a welcome and a promise
of ultimate surrender. Oh
how cunningly she urged them on
to frenzy only then to fight
them off with righteous indignation!
Phony. That was the word for it.
And no less phony when she fell
for Stuart and his motorcycle.
By winding country roads with cows
and whitewashed ranches under rows
of eucalyptus trees they came
to apple orchards and the trunks
of redwoods rising up beyond.
There stood a cabin hidden deep
in shadow under trees so huge
their tops were lost, yet windows showed
the sunwashed valley and the blue
of mountains all along the east.
They drew a bearskin to the fire
and kissed long kisses there and then
they went to bed together. Chaste

were their embraces. Hard indeed
the trial but no veil was rent
whatever else they did. Her Stuart
painted as a pastime. Long
he begged her to become his model
till she who was ashamed to walk
unclad across her room alone
at last consented. Stripped to bra
and pants she posed. Further she could
not bring herself to go. Yet all
exultant was she when she saw
her lovely shape emerge on canvas.
When Stuart finished it she turned
on sudden impulse and embraced him.
"Take me now!" she said, "right now!"
"No, dear," he said. "I have too much
respect for you. We've gone this long
without it. Soon I'll be in service.
When I come back perhaps we'll see
our way. I wouldn't want to hurt you."
What anticlimax! After all
the men she'd thwarted and sent slinking
homeward like beaten curs from jousts
with her, to love a man at last
enough to give herself completely
and find herself rejected! Humbled
she got into her clothes again.
An Air Force captain was the next,
a prancing man who drove his car
as if it were the jet he flew.
This time her love was quick to flower
but smarting still from Stuart's snub
she played it cautious and outdid
her former self in that old game.
The amorous captain was enraged
to find himself incompetent
for once against a female who
admired him. Stung, he sought to force
her in a lonely parking place.
Failing in this he seized her head
in both his hands and forced it down
into his lap. The burst of fluid
slimed her face.

                              Lew spoke again,
"I'm sorry I talked that way to you."
"You needn't be," she answered him.
"It makes me mad sometimes," he said,
"the airs you women give yourselves.
And then I blow my stack and say
the kind of things I wish I hadn't
afterwards. I don't know why
I brought you here to Santa Cruz.
I'm no good for anybody.
You better keep the hell away."
How fast the man could change his line!
And yet he looked sincere, the face
all darkly brooding with its shame,
big shoulders hunched and downcast, hands
tight-twisted in the sand. Her heart
went out to him somehow. She reached
and put a hand on his two. "Take
it easy, Lew, you've had it rough
I know. Don't blame yourself too much.
You aren't the worst man in the world."
"The trouble is," he said, "no woman
has ever understood me like
you seem to do. They drove me wild.
My mom, she never liked me. Sis
was always right and I was wrong.
I moved away from home with Dad
when he pulled out on Mom and then
I got in with a gang. One day
a couple of us found a car
unlocked. I was fifteen. We picked
some girls up. Headed north for Portland.
We made it to Yreka. There
the girls got scared and turned us in.
They accused us two of raping them
to fix things with their folks. The cops,
they beat us in the county jail
with leather belts, the buckle end,
till we confessed. They left us there
with rats and flying cockroaches
that lit upon your face at night
and when you waked up yelling
they came and put you back to sleep

with buckle ends. They shipped us back
at last to juvenile detention.
That was the place you learned to be
somebody's punk until your turn
came up to make some littler guy
play punk for you. The kids had knives
and bludgeons in the cell blocks. Used
them too. And there they taught you all
you might not know about the ways
there are of stealing cars and rolling
queers and every kind of racket.
When I got out I practiced all
I'd learned. For close to 18 years
I kept it up. I guess my sis
has briefed you on her no-good brother."
"She told me you were dangerous."
"A big help she is," and he smiled.
"Weren't you paroled to her?"
                             "That's right."
"Doesn't she keep you on the payroll
to cover up for you?"
                    He scowled.
"Who gave you all this crap?"
                        "She did.
Why? Isn't it the truth?"
                      "I guess
it is," he said despondently.
"I told you once to stay away.
Why are you keeping after me?"
"Because you need someone," she said,
"who'll love you. No one ever did.
That's all the trouble with you, Lew."

II

The light was burning in the parlor
when they drove up to where she lived,
a house like all the others in
the Sunset district. Fog was thick.
The street was like a tunnel. Home
and Mama waiting up to question
her wandering daughter. Who had she
been out with this time? Where might they
have been until the wee small hours?
And when she went to bed and seemed
asleep then Mama might steal in
to search for evidence upon
her underthings. So Margaret
took leave of Lew below. "No, no,"
she told him when he sought to hold
her in a last embrace. "She saw
the car drive up. She's watching us
behind the curtains. Let me go.
Call me at work." She broke away
and hurried up the steps in front.
The door came open and her brother
stood weaving there. "Why George!" she said,
"What keeps you waiting up?"
                                    "You do,"
he said with drunken righteousness.
Inside she saw the heap of beer cans
they'd killed between them. Mama too
was high. She glowered from her chair.
"Now Margaret," her mother said,
"no use to lie to us. We know
who you were out with. He's no good.
Georgie found out about him. Frank
Gilhooley saw you two together
and he told Georgie if he cared
about his sister's character

he wouldn't let her run around
with an ex-convict."
                              Margaret
sat down. "I'm not discussing Lew,"
she said. "You can't tell me a thing
about him I don't know. It's my
affair. I don't need George or Frank
or any other brassrail heroes
for my protectors. I'm of age.
And if I want to throw myself
away on Lew I will."
                              "You will?"
said George. "You'll bring disgrace down on
your family? Do you expect
we're going to stand for that?"
                              "Your dad,"
Mama said sniffling, "wouldn't have stood
for it. If he was living you
can bet he'd kill this fellow Lew.
Your dad would kill him with his fists.
And you he'd take across his knee.
You wouldn't sit down for a week."
With golden stripes that showed his rating,
Chief Boatswain's Mate, was how
her dad came back to mind, a man
who could do anything she asked,
fix skates or bicycle or teach
her how to kick a football like
a boy. How he had made her wish
she really was a boy! How hard
she'd tried to be a better one
than George! Scabs always on her knees
from wrestling with him on the walk.
Mama would moan. Dad said he wished
that George had half her guts.
                              George poured
himself another can of beer.
"You have your choice," he said. "It's him
or us. You can't live here and run
around with convicts." Quaffing down
the beer he wiped his mouth and belched.
"You mean this, George?" asked Margaret.
"You really mean it? Have you thought

it over? Sober up and try
to figure how you'll get along
without the money I bring home."
"Mama and I can get along,"
he shouted. "We don't need your help.
We'd rather be on charity
than take your dirty money. How
much does he give you for it? Ten
or is it twenty dollars now?"
"Georgie," her mother said, "lay off
of Margaret. The girl's not bad.
Just foolish."

                    She had made her mind
up long ago but hadn't known
how she could leave them. Now they made
it easy for her. "Mama, this
is it. I've had it. Keep the house.
You two are welcome to my share.
I'm getting out." She ran into
her room and slammed the door and packed
a suitcase. Coming out she saw
them both incredulously staring
with glasses in their hands. "Goodbye,"
she said.

               "You can't do this to us,"
her mother said. "Besides, where will
you go at two o'clock at night?"
"There are hotels," she answered. Then
for spite she added, "and there's Lew."

Outside the foghorns from the ocean
kept up a hoarse and steady blare.
Shivering she walked to Judah.
The streaks of neon blurred and bled
for empty block on block. A car
pulled up alongside sleek and black.
"Going places, babe?"

                      "No thank you,"
she replied but still he stuck,
cruising slowly as she walked.
"I got a thing here," came the voice,
"I'd like to show you."

                              Quick she ducked
into a phone booth by a closed
gas station. He who had accosted
her took off with sudden roar
of twin exhausts. She found the number.
"The Golden Calf" on Mission Street.
Lew's sister owned the place. He hung
out there and sometimes tended bar.
Lew answered, "Margaret?" He seemed
amused. "What is the matter, doll?"
What was the matter? Why hadn't she
called Alma? Alma lived just off
the carline on Parnassus Street.
Alma would take her in until
tomorrow. "Nothing really. I got
a scare. Some jerk in one of these
hopped-up Mercuries made like
a wolf. He's gone."
                      "Aren't you at home?"
"We had a quarrel. George was up.
He threw me out. All over you."
"Where are you?"
                      "Thirtieth and Judah."
"I'm coming over."
                      "You needn't, Lew.
My girl friend lives up on Parnassus.
I'll stay with her."
                      "You wait right there."

Somehow they never got to Alma's.
Blue windows shone against the fog
where surgeons worked to save a life
and then Parnassus dropped behind.
Their headlights did not penetrate
the soupy night. She shrank against
Lew's shoulder as they sped downtown.
They ended at a tenderloin
hotel on Turk off Market. Where
else could she go? Why argue now?
"Hi Lew," the nightclerk said. So he
was known here. In a lobby chair
a girl was sitting by herself.

The girl looked up and smiled. Too red
her lips were and the teeth she bared
were also smeared with red like tusks.
Lew pulled a roll of bills and peeled
off one. The clerk took down a key
that hung upon a board. Lew signed
the register. "Mr. and Mrs.
Joe Blow, Los Angeles, Calif."
The carpet on the stairs was ragged.
  Why have you brought me here? You know
I won't give in to you. Not here.
Not in a place like this."
                                    "I know,"
he said. "You have to go where they
will take you in. That's all. We'll move
tomorrow."
              "We'll move?"
                            "You'll move then.
I didn't mean a thing by that."
                                The room
smelled urinous. The bed was bowed
with overwork. A single bulb
flyspecked and dim hung down and lit
the place. The filthy window faced
the blackness of a shaft down which
a maudlin voice began to sing.
"Shut up, you bitch!" rang out and all
was silence once again.
                            "Please go,"
she told him but he only swept
her up and laid her on the bed.
"Oh Lew," she said, "I'm tired. Please
leave me alone." His mouth crushed out
her words and hands began to move
among her clothes. What was the use?
Why had she struggled for so long?
What did it matter after all?
"Lew, don't," she whispered, then, "Oh Lew,
you will be careful. Please be careful."
He had undressed her. "Turn the light
out," was her only plea. He did
and soon his naked weight bestrode
her prostrate body. Panic fear

beset her and she wildly moaned,
locking her legs together. "Please,"
he begged her, "open up a little."
"You won't do anything?" she sobbed.
"You're sure you won't?"
                              "I won't.
Honest I won't."
                    The pain transfixed
her like a flaming spear. Too proud
to scream she bit her lips and writhed.
He held her in a brutal clutch
and she could feel his moving warmth
inside her. "Stop!" she pleaded. "Stop!"
At last he stopped and lay beside
her breathing heavily. "You didn't?"
she asked him, "didn't finish in me?"
"No."
          "You're sure?"
                              "I swear I didn't."
"Thank you for that at least. I think
you must have hurt me pretty bad.
I feel all wet. Turn on the light."
He turned it on. There in the beams
of that one solitary bulb
she saw beneath her on the sheet
a spreading pool of her own blood.

III

It couldn't be. And yet it was.
The doctor said so. She was pregnant.
"My God!" he said. "You say you knew
this man? He tore you so. You're sure
you knew him?"
                            "Yes," she said.
                                        And now
she really knew him all the way.
"You lied about not finishing?"
she asked Lew. "I guess so," he said.
"I was afraid to tell you then."
He hung his head. "What you expect
a man to do?"
                            "Not lie."
                                        He laughed
a sheepish laugh. "I'll fix you up,"
he said. "But not so loud. My sis
is in the back." He turned and poured
himself a straight one, gulped it down
and said, "I know a doc who does
abortions for $400.
I could get up the cash for you."
"You'll have to marry me," she said
and loathing of him made her gag.
"You wouldn't have to live with me.
Just marry me."
                            "Jeez, that's a hot
one. Don't you think I got enough
raps hanging over me without
committing bigamy?"
                            "You told
me you were single, Lew."
                                        "I'm not,"
he said and scowled. "I got a frau
in Phoenix. And two kids. She don't

know where I am. And she don't care
I guess. She makes good money now.
But she won't give me a divorce.
She said she didn't want to see
me louse up any other woman's
life. She said she'd drop the boom
on me if she should ever hear
I'd married anybody else."
"Pour me a drink, Lew, or I'll faint."
She put her head down on the bar.
Round and round she spun. The shot
revived her. Calm, she told herself,
she must be calm or else this man
would manufacture some excuse
for ditching her as he had ditched
his wife. "Abortion, Lew!" she said.
"How could I do a thing like that?"
"There's nothing to it." Leaning toward
her in his barkeep's apron he
turned on his boyish charm and said,
"It's just like taking off a wart."
Her mind grew clear at last. She'd tried
hot mustard baths and even let
herself fall down a flight of stairs.
The sin was in the will and she
had willed to kill the baby. What
would be the good of having it'
in some hide-out for wayward girls?
Her mother would discover it
and so would George and never would
she hear the end of it. If only
they'd let her keep her baby. No.
For she would never even see
the child she bore. Those places put
the babies out at birth to be
adopted.
            "OK, Lew," she said.
"Arrange it."
                        Promises were all
she got from him. Each time the deal
fell through. The doc backed out he said.
Or else he didn't have the cash
right then. A month went by. At last

she cornered him and said she'd turn
him in to the police unless
he came across. The date was made
he said. The doc was set. He'd get
the cash and meet her after work
in front of Old St. Mary's church.
Two hours she watched the tower clock
where underneath was written, SON,
OBSERVE THE TIME AND FLY FROM EVIL.
The darkness fell and still no Lew.
She went inside the church and tried
to pray. Her heart was dead and dry.
A priest was hearing in the box.
Tomorrow was First Friday. How
could she confess her frightful sins?
Once Mama caught her in the basement.
The boy next door and she were playing
doctor. It was an awful sin,
her mama said, and God might strike
her dead. She was polluted in
His sight and must be cleansed at once.
Her mama took her then and there
to make confession. She had lied
and told the priest the boy had seen
her thighs by accident. How could
you tell a thing so shameful even
if you should burn in hell forever?
She crossed herself and left the church.

"No," Lew's sister answered when
she phoned the bar. "Lew isn't here.
He went to Tanforan to play
the horses. Shall I say you called?"
"No." She hung up. So he had known
she wouldn't carry out her threat.
What good to put him back in prison?
Her secret would be out. No help
would come from him. Not now. Not ever.
Poor Mr. Kieck! Why should she think
of Mr. Kieck just now? What could
he do? That scarecrow man with arms
that jutted from his sleeves and neck
with adam's apple jumping up

and down from feeling when he read
out loud a poem he liked or theme
some student in the class had written.
How they had laughed at him but she
had almost loved the man that year
she took his course and he'd responded
absurdly in his fashion. She
had written things he liked about
her life. He called her "Desdemona."
"My Desdemona" sometimes. Now
she might claim kinship with that girl
slain in her bed but then it seemed
so funny. Mr. Kieck was forty
with wife and children in a flat
on Clipper Street up from Dolores.
He walked to school to save a dime
in cracked old army shoes. His pants
were frayed along the cuffs and shone
behind. They said he was some kind
of radical and she had heard
he wouldn't sign some oath or other
they asked him to, and lost his job.
Maybe poor Mr. Kieck had need
for help himself. How could she ask him?
She sat in Old St. Mary's Square
and watched the lights like shooting stars
of cars that crossed the Oakland bridge.
She could jump off or better yet
take sleeping pills. Suppose though that
they didn't work and she came to
again? You read about that happening.
What could she do to make it sure?
And who would care in all the world?
Poor Mr. Kieck might care. She rose.
There was a taxi at the stand.
"Take me to Clipper Street," she said,
"up from Dolores." Over the noise
of second gear the driver heard
such weeping that he floored the gas.

IV

"You can't blame anyone for what
he does," said Mr. Kieck, "not even
a man like Lew. Where would he learn?
The modern jungle was his school,
the slum, the broken home, the jail,
the whore house and the crooked track.
You hurt or get hurt, that's the law
of that harsh lawless world."

       "I blame
myself," she said. "I should have known.
Now this. I'm so ashamed."

       She bowed
her head. A trailer truck swerved past
with blast of airhorn and black plume
of diesel smoke. The ancient car
that Mr. Kieck had bought for fifty
dollars to pack his brushes in
upon his rounds from house to house
was hardly fit for freeway traffic.
On Visitacion he turned off
and drove on slowly reading numbers.
It was a corner place with lawn
and flowers. Two new Cadillacs
stood in the carport. Under the bell
a plaque read RING. An eye looked through
a peephole at them. Then a nurse
unlocked the door and led them in.
She sat down at a desk beneath
a gilded mirror. "Please pay now,"
she said. "The fee will be $400.
We don't take checks." Then Margaret
passed over twenty 20's with
a rubber band around them, just
as Mr. Kieck had got them from
the bookstore where he sold his books.

"I need the space," he'd said. "Maybe
I'll teach again some day and then
I'll buy them back. I don't need books
to sell the housewife brushes." She
remembered how the naked shelves
had looked in that dark flat on Clipper
up from Dolores. Mrs. Kieck
had brought her tea, a homely woman
but with a smile that was as if
a light went on behind her face.
The two small Kiecks had sat all eyes
and watched her drink her tea until
she choked on it and had to lie
down on the faded Chesterfield.
"Doctor will see you now." A masked
and white-gowned man was waiting by
a gleaming obstetrician's table.
The nurse helped Margaret undress
behind a screen and put her in
a backless gown, then lifted her
up on the table. Instruments
were ready in a tray. Her thighs
were thrust apart and clamped and then
she felt the glittering steel make entrance.

When Margaret came out she saw
a strange girl in the gilded mirror
with horror-stricken eyes and lips
all bloodless in a chalky face.
And then she knew herself. "I am
that guilty thing that looks at me,"
she thought. "I am that murderess
who killed the life within her womb."
Poor Mr. Kieck got up and took
her arm. They started out. She watched
the tears run down his nose and drop.
They made a trail along the rug.

VI

POEMS
1955–1960

THE IRON MAIDEN

Sometimes along palazzo corridors
or in the echoing vaults of castle keeps
or cold stone dungeons underneath the ground
among the torture wheels and windlasses
the thumbscrews and the monstrous metal boots
where molten lead was poured and out came foot
scoured whistle clean of flesh and tendon-strings
there you chance to see the iron maiden
black with antique rust and bloodcaked too
you fancy as you finger thrusting spikes

Demure and chaste her moulded face appears
the upright breasts declaring her a maiden
her supple figure draped in lines that cling
concealing nothing really worth revealing
save the hideous reality
couched within that hinged exterior
Once swung open and a man shoved in
manacled and gagged against his screams
the maiden clanged together and her spikes
gouged eyeballs out and speared his flesh all over

What a distance we have come from days
when barbarous implements like these were used
to enforce a uniformity of view
on those who doubted or were thought to doubt
the reigning imbecility of belief!
Now probes and oaths suffice to tame and curb
the unquiet questing spirit and should these fail
his relatives and friends will spy upon him
reporting all he says or thinks and last
the blacklist slowly buries him alive

TO ALEXANDER MEIKLEJOHN
On the Occasion of His Senate Testimony
in Defense of Liberty

I read your testimony and I thought
here is the man perfected that I knew
and reverenced next him who gave me life.
Too soon the long black limousine will stand
before your door and all unhearing you
will trundle off on casters while the winds
of elegiac oratory fill
the public prints and how the hearts will ache
of us who were your sons. Too late we'll carve
your stone. The time is now for rising up
and speaking out our love. Know then, dear man,
that mine has grown beyond the hero worship
of youth when your ideas broke the mould
of prejudice in which my mind was formed.
You let the world in on me, were the yeast
that set me boiling with desire to know
not merely but to do. I thought I loved
my country. You taught why America
deserved my love and all mankind's because
America was more than just a land;
it was the sum of all that men had won
against the ancient darkness. So believing
my life grew meaningful and where before
I felt myself an atom in the void
I now engaged to join with other men
to keep the light alive and specially
to oppose all those who in the name of light
would re-enthrone the darkness and betray
America. This they have nearly done.
And I myself in prime of life have felt
the anguished bitterness that exiles know
cut off and cast away. How easy now
to curse America, cast in one's lot
with enemies, back one usurping gang
against the other! But for you I think
I would have made this all-too-human error.
Despised, rejected as I felt, the thought
of you restrained me at the brink. "What would

he think? What would he do himself?" So clear
the answer always came. "Believe!" you said,
"Don't let them drive you to despair! Fight on!"

SCREENED

Most mornings you will find him
perched on the ledge beside the library
where homeless men foregather in the sun
like hungry crows along a fence
waiting for what they know by now
will never come

Around noon he leaves his perch
and heads toward Saint Anthony's to stand
with hat in hand for stew and beans
and afterwards he takes his daily walk
down the Embarcadero where
the ships are berthed

His destination is the tower
on Telegraph Hill and there he sits
all afternoon upon the parapet
watching the movement in the harbor
oblivious to the tourists
who stare at him

Among the gleaming cars the cameras
the sport togs and the jewelry
of elegant women he strikes a jarring note
in frayed and slept-in clothes
and people wonder why the police
don't move him on

It is a wonder that they don't
Perhaps they know how useless it would be
for by tomorrow they'd see him there again

or it may even be they still remember
what those pins on his lapel
were given for

Three torpedoes made of silver
meaning this man abandoned ship
that many times when wolf-packs roamed the sea
Some shipmates drowned some fried in oil
while some cracked up beside him
in the lifeboat

This man survived three sinkings
His grateful country then awarded him
three small torpedo pins for his lapel
and when the war was over
reviewed his seaman's papers secretly
and put him on the beach

Informants who for reasons of security
must remain anonymous avouched
that subject was suspected of subversive
leanings by his captain on one voyage
and was reported to have said he'd like
to visit Russia

Subject also was alleged
to have been prematurely anti-fascist
It was believed he'd had a hand one time
in hauling down the Nazi swastika
flying from a ship in port for which
police had clubbed him

And so the gold braid screened him off the ships
He asked to hear the charges and was told
the charges were a secret but if he
could guess them and reply thereto
his affidavit would receive
consideration

Thirty years at sea were thus
without redress or legal process ended
and since the man possessed no property
or trade beside the skill of seamanship

he became the public pauper
whom we observe

He sits upon the parapet
and follows with his eyes a ship
long gray and fleet that through the Golden Gate
makes way toward the open sea
The sunset burnishes the silver pins
on his lapel

REFLECTIONS OF A MAN WHO ONCE STOOD UP FOR FREEDOM

I'd say that gesture cost enough
but who can reckon up these things?
I'll hardly live to see the day
when I'll be justified at last
if ever that day comes. I wonder
often whether this is not
the onset of an age of darkness
covering all the earth. Could we
be quarantined against a plague
which saturates the atmosphere
we breathe and must continue breathing?
The world is indivisible
and so is freedom. Force and fraud
employed to scuttle human rights
in Spain or China, Mississippi
or Morocco, surely do
reverberate around the world.
They make the climate of our time
as certainly as when a storm
engendered in Siberia
with drifted snow can paralyze
New York and blast the orange crop

in Florida. Well, you might say
that it was my supreme misfortune
to recognize what kind of storm
was bearing down upon us. I sought
to warn the rest of you, for which
no thanks to me. The Jeremiah
role is rarely popular.
And so I got the old heave-ho
from my profession as perhaps
I should have known and after that
I found myself an outcast. Friends
quite naturally avoided me
lest my unclean touch defile them
and when I tried to find a job
all doors were closed against me. "Why,
it would be easier to place
a convict on parole than you!"
they told me at the office where
I went to seek employment. Then
my son quit college and my daughter
also. She'd wanted to be a teacher
like me. She's now a secretary
while my son, embittered, drifts
from job to job. Their mother failed
to appreciate my heroism.
Quixotic was the kindest term
she found for my behavior. First
we separated. After that
divorce was natural. We'd been
so close for more than twenty years!
She couldn't understand of course
and, do you know, sometimes I can't.
I really don't know why I threw
my life away for principle.
It seems an empty thing from here
shoveling behind these cows.

OBSERVATIONS ON A GUIDED TOUR

We landed at Boston
one of their oldest towns
rich in monuments of greatness
We were driven to Bunker Hill
visited Lexington and Concord
saw the homes of Emerson
Thoreau and Lowell
champions they told us
of free speech and kindred errors
Afterwards we went to pay respects
to His Eminence
who favored us with a brief address
of greeting to America
Affairs were well in hand he indicated
No book was sold or cinema was shown
without his chancery's approval
Tradition was a stubborn thing he said
and Boston had been the lair
of pernicious liberalism once
but this by slow degrees had given way
to authority and orthodoxy
The faithful have the votes he said
to keep such men in office
as We in Our wisdom designate
We thanked His Eminence for throwing light
on how democracy works in Boston
and went aboard a bus for Plymouth Rock

CLIMATE OF FEAR

She was so emotional about it
I tried to tell her but she wouldn't listen
she ought to take these things in stride
and not get bothered
but you know how she was about the oath

That's all she talked about for months
and how when she got her credential
she'd make her living picking apples
before she'd sign the oath and teach
She told me once that she had joined
some group or other and when she found
it wasn't democratic she got out
and then it turned up on a list
That's why she carried on about the oath
She was afraid to sign
but all the same she did
That was just talk about the apples
She signed the oath and got a job
teaching in a little country school
and then one day she turned up here
frothing at the mouth
They were after her she said
Who? I asked her
Some parent in her school
had denounced her to the Board
because she talked about the Bill of Rights
in class one day and said that she believed
we didn't have the freedom we used to have
The Board was mostly ranchers
who've been fighting with the union up there
You probably read about them beating up
that organizer with a chain
They thought she must have meant them
so they got hot and called the FBI
Some agent from the city came and quizzed her
about her associations and so forth
He knew all about this thing
she once belonged to
and he kept asking her for names
but she refused to give him any
She was so frightened she was shaking still
She told me she was positive
she'd lose her job and then be prosecuted
because she'd signed the oath and in the end
she'd go to jail for perjury
I told her she was overwrought
and just imagining all that
I said let's go take in a show

but she rushed off again
Next thing I heard they'd found her car
parked by the bridge

OUR THOUGHTS ARE FREE

Listen!
Ralph is going to sing for us
Die Gedanken sind frei
Oh that's the one I love so much
It means *Our thoughts are free*
Such a message for today!
Look there at those Williamses!
What gall of them to come!
They claim they can't afford a contribution
to our club this year
and yet they have the nerve
to show their faces at our picnic!
Did you hear what Bunny Williams said
to Miriam?
She told Miriam she thought our country
was not the only one to blame for wars
around the world the atom race and all
She said the Soviet Union was almost
as bad as we are
Yes she did!
That's exactly what she said
Her husband Henry's just as anti-everything
as Bunny is
The government purged him from his job
because he'd fought in Spain
the International Brigade you know
and now he's selling hearing aids
but Paul believes that's just a blind
Paul put out the word to keep away
from Henry Williams

Paul heard him criticize the Party once
and hasn't trusted him for years
Paul says those hearing aids
that Henry carries in that bag of his
to make you think he sells them
probably are hidden dictaphones
that take down every word you say
Don't even speak to him
the dirty stool-pigeon!
Oh Ralph that song was so inspiring!
Encore! Encore!

THE SEARCH FOR TRUTH

Do I have freedom here
to search for truth and teach it to my students
the way I used to
before the oath and all these things came in?
Freedom is such a nebulous word
I don't know what you mean exactly
You'd have to define your terms
I teach the way I always have
but you know how it is
one goes on learning
one grows more experienced
one's taste becomes more disciplined
one realizes that the young
are prone to take things literally
and so a gradual approach to truth
is sometimes indicated
It seems to me a choice of values
is involved in this whole question
of so-called academic freedom
The public hires us to teach the young
Well and good
Would it then be fair for us

to betray the public trust
and teach our students what the public
does not approve of?
Clearly not and furthermore
we are dependent on the public
for our support
At last our salaries begin to match
those of professionals in other fields
and should we jeopardize these gains
with ill-conceived quixotic claims
to be a law unto ourselves?
Each year the legislature votes for us
another three per cent increase in pay
and look around you at these buildings
our new gymnasium our stadium
These mean we have the public's confidence
I wouldn't want to see this sacrificed
I don't think you would either
My attitude about the Mitchell case?
My opinion is that Dr. Mitchell
for all his undoubted brilliance
is not a man of tact and showed less judgment
than a full professor should possess
The police force as we know is far from honest
riddled with corruption if you please
What city's force is any better?
But to send one's students over town
sticking their noses into everything
with questionnaires
not even leaving out the brothels!
This was too much
He put the institution and his colleagues
to use a vulgar term upon the spot
with that investigation of the links
between police and prostitutes
That kind of thing is not our business
We should concern ourselves
with the eternal verities
and not the ephemeral passing show
We see events in true perspective only
generations after they occur
and all this hue and cry
over academic freedom

will surely seem a tempest in a teapot
a century or two from now
Of course it is a shame that Dr. Mitchell
had to go
He'd published many books
and was a credit to the faculty
May you quote me?
Oh no indeed!
I meant no criticism by my remark
It was a wise decision to dismiss him
I just meant . . .
Really I didn't mean a thing
but Mitchell was my friend
Don't quote me though
I want that off the record

ALTER CHRISTUS

Yes I remember him
a truly saintly priest
alter Christus
that is to say *another Christ*
such as we priests are all supposed to be
but yet you know a man like that
can do more mischief than a hundred
of the humdrum usual kind
That trouble he got into
could so easily have been avoided
Foolhardy was the word for him
I remember how for years he set his face
against all plans of his parishioners
to provide him with a car and driver
The Twelve Disciples went on foot he said
so trolleys should be good enough for him
Off he'd go to nowhere on the trolley
all alone and in the dead of night

taking the sacraments to some poor soul
regardless of the danger that he ran
The Ku Klux Klan was capable
of luring him to some abode of vice
on a fake call
and compromising him in people's eyes
thus doing all us priests an injury
The Bishop tried to make him see
the folly of his ways but he
just shook his head and smiled angelically
No harm could come to him he said
on such a holy errand
Our Lord Himself was there to guard him
How innocently trusting he could be!
So when this woman came to him and said
she'd like him to instruct her in the faith
he went ahead despite her character
Why she was a fallen woman
a very Magdalen!
He should have been more prudent
but no he treated her as if she'd been
a bona fide convert
and found a husband for her in the Church
Some kind of foreigner
I never went along with those who claimed
the foreigner had Negro blood
though to be sure his skin was rather swarthy
but still the woman's father had good cause
to feel aggrieved
He was a Klansman
a sort of jackleg preacher
who hung around the court house
and eked a living out by marrying couples
hot off the license bureau
Perhaps he felt his business was infringed
Right in broad day he took his gun
The priest was sitting on his porch
reading his breviary for Passion Week
and hearing feet come up the steps
he must have raised his eyes
and looked into the pistol's mouth
Some might consider him a martyr
but do you know

he actually did us all a lot of harm
The murderer was acquitted of his crime
by a jury packed with Klansmen
and the woman didn't even stick
She fell away soon afterwards
They always do that kind
The town believed that there had been
something between the two of them
The whisper went around
and where a priest's involved
such whispers find a ready ear
That's why I always say
we can't be too suspicious
of those who come to us
from lives of public vice and sin
with tears of feigned repentance
The safest thing for us to do
is shut our door against such persons
lest scandal enter in

AN AIR THAT KILLS

Times were worse then /
Jobs were hard to get /
People were suffering more /
but do you know
a man could breathe //

It's as if the oxygen
were all exhausted
from the atmosphere //
That's how I feel /
and why I quit //

Same land / same sky / same sea /
same trees and mountains //

I painted then/
I guess the light went out
I saw them by //

Don't make politics
out of what I say/
It's just that something isn't here
that used to be
and kept us going//

THE BETTER SORT OF PEOPLE

Our Negroes here are satisfied
They don't complain about a thing
except the weather maybe
whenever it's too cold to fish
for cat along the riverbank
But when they get away from here
up to Chicago or Detroit
and stay a while and then come back with notions
about the right to vote
or going to school with white folks
we sometimes have to get it through their heads
who runs this country
They're better off down here
or else why don't they stay up yonder?
A lot of them keep coming back
but somehow they've been spoiled
and need the fear of God
thrown into them again
Mind you I'm against the kind of thing
the ignorant rednecks do
I think it was unnecessary
to beat that little Negro boy to death
and throw his body in the Tallahatchie

He was uppity
no doubt about it
and whistled at a white woman
He probably learned that in Chicago
so we ought to make allowances
A good horsewhipping should have been enough
to put him back into his place
and been sufficient warning to him that
if ever he got fresh again
he wouldn't live to see Chicago
Those rednecks that abducted him
I doubt if even they
really meant to kill him when they started
working on him
They just got too enthusiastic
Like I say the better sort of people
down here in Mississippi
we love our Negroes
We wouldn't harm them for the world
This violence you hear so much about
is all the fault of low-down rednecks
poor white trash

TURN OF THE YEAR

Sea-serpents churn the sky and octopi
twine slimy tentacles about the firs.
Aleutian-bred, the equinoctial storm
abolishes that composition all
cerulean and gold which summer brushed
upon the coastal ranges. Raging gusts
squander the coinage of my Royal Annes,
minted but yesterday. A glint of sun
flees down the slopes and vanishes like fawns
startled among the apples—a dappled flash

and over the fence into the redwood grove.
Siva, destruction's king, was multi-limbed
as these sequoias, choreographers
of death, aghast against the stricken sky.

Morning Star Ranch, Sebastopol California, 1956

BROTHER INNOCENT

Within your cloister
Brother Innocent
you beat your breast I know
for pagan days of yours when flesh was hot
and spilled itself in poems
concupiscent and unashamed
in front of all the world

Now
you make amends with nights upon your knees
where one small flame in all the darkness
burns before the sacred host
and days you spend in lowly ways
abased within your category
answering the bells
of monks whose sum of talent
comes to scarce a tithe of yours

Thought and act were one with you
even in days gone by
before the vision broke upon you
Murder was murder
your conscience said
in war as well as peace
and no fine words of prelate or of President
could make you see it otherwise
You bore no hand in slaughter
but chose instead a labor camp

Worse jails there could have been
but still
you were not free to leave
and when you were at last
five years had fled away
and women being what they are
flesh frail as yours or mine
you found your wife had been
well solaced in your absence

As pagans are wont to do
you left her
and took unto yourself another
who in her turn had been deceived
as you were cuckolded
Together you sought to wipe away
the tears of things
from one another's eyes
as if two people ever could

More sad your partner grew
and seeking out a healer of the mind
learned that her sickness lodged in guilt
for childhood faith forsaken
He counseled her to pluck
this buried faith up by the roots
like some choking weed
and burn it in the fire of reason
Instead she nourished it to bloom once more
and speedily grew well

And so a second time
you lost a wife
or did you only seem to lose her?
You found like refuge in the eternal rock
and ever deeper delve inside
as one who fleeing Caesar
threads labyrinths of catacombs
with holy taper guiding him
while in his ears
the Colosseum's muffled roars resound

A DEATH AT SEA

Off Jupiter light we rolled our beams
till Gulfstream indigo supplanted green swells.
Line paid out, the club-thick rod fast-socketed,
the wicked lure thrashed up
a witching rainbow in our wake.
The sailfish when she struck careened me to the rail,
line screaming the reel. Enginewards the skipper
leaped churning his craft astern.
Reeling in, I felt the sailfish rage for liberty
as if electric shock ran through my bones,
and when she jumped
her parabolic fin flashed nacreous in the sun.
We fought an hour upon that indigo sea
until I staggered on the deck
gulping for breath and she
lay lashing wearied by the stern.
The gaff bit deep into her iridescent side
and she shone an instant like a captured mermaid in the air
but in a frenzied spasm
tore her flesh free from hooks and gaff
and dove to die in her own element.

THE SHORE OF PEACE

War called you from the mill
whence come those powerful hands and frame
that make men fear you when you wish
the measured gait as if you balanced
heavy beams upon your shoulders
and roughened face
like iron cast in sand

You drove a tank
in all that clanking troop
that rolled a storm of dust

across Tunisia's desert hills
toward the shore where Carthage stood
before the Romans rooted out
that rival city
and salted down the ground
lest dragon's teeth once more
should spring up there

A score of centuries
and who could count the wars
since chariot wheels of Scipio Africanus
dug ruts where now your whirling tracks
churned through the alkali
but when you reached the narrow pass
foes broke from ambush and with fire
of mobile guns blasted your column
The medics found you crushed
and burned beside your gutted tank

But not so crushed nor yet so burned
that you were privileged to die
Your native strength and all the arts
whereby we drag men back from death
so they may live to kill again
these saved you and restored you

That shore you then assaulted
where once the youth of Athens came
wading from their galleys through the surf
They were the lucky ones who died
beneath the Syracusan swords
The rest wore chains and quarried stone
until the alien sun
bleached out their graveless bones

Life-jacketed you stood on deck
in the lee of that hostile coast
when sudden wings screamed down
and LST joined Greek trireme
below
Among the bodies washed ashore
was yours

but once again
your pulse kept shuddering on

And once again
the surgeons sutured and trepanned
with rubber-fingered skill
until they could pronounce you fit
for bloody work
and such you did along a road to Rome
that barefoot pilgrims used to walk

You helped obliterate
that hallowed abbey on its crag
the motherhouse of all the west
where Benedict himself had walked
in meditation on his Holy Rule
but our guns in blasphemous choir
chanted the hour of compline there
and *Consummatum est* was heard once more
beneath a blackened sky

From Germany laid waste
victorious you sailed for home
Home was the same but you were not
The vacant talk of friends
the well-filled envelope of weekly cash
the soothing flesh of women
none of these assuaged
the deep hurt in you
that for all their scopes and rays
the doctors could not diagnose

You found asylum then
where Wasatch peaks at evening
throw shadows on the fields of hay
You moved among the silent brothers
robed and cowled in coarsest brown
about your tasks in scullery and barn
as Benedict had bidden

Straw upon a board your bed
your fare but bread and barley water

with green stuff from the garden
Long before the dawn you rose
and after lauds and matins sung
fasting still you labored
while stars yet shone
with all the lustre of the Utah night

A year this was your world entire
a universe removed from men
and men's concern for self
In all that while you spoke no word
save to confess your faults
Milking cows or dunging fields
your every act was prayer as deep
as psalms the choir monks chanted
within their carven stalls

What made you lay aside
your hooded Trappist habit?
What fiery-sworded angel
or was it conscience that forbade
you any longer to inhabit
this austere paradise?

You chose to make your home
with those who have no homes
the castaways of modern life
who in the roaring city are more lone
than hermits in their fastnesses
Immured are these each in his private hell
as on the flames they pour
the fuel alcohol and burn
themselves to deathlike sleep and wake
to pour and burn and die afresh

These sodden men
these women all degraded
you feed
as they file by with hanging heads
Each day you make the rounds
and beg on their behalf
stale loaves

fishes that stink
whatever men can't sell

From that same dish
whereon the wretched feed
you dine
That flophouse where they lay
their drunken heads each night
is also your hotel
Within your lumpy bed
you even share their bugs

And when one stifling afternoon
outside the Silver Dollar Bar
Willie the Weeper flips his lid
and shouts upon his knees
for God to strike him dead
while all his reeling cohorts circle
jeering round him on the sidewalk
you are the one who shoulders through the ring
to lift poor Willie up
and bear him tenderly away

BODEGA HEAD
For Barbara

On these miles of sand the cold sea beats
watched only by me as I walk
Wheeling around me the gulls
lustfully shriek over corpses of fish
washed up by the poisonous waters
Ship's timbers all shivered and wan
lie about on the beach and stir into mind
the death of a schooner on the offshore reef

Borne here across infinite ocean
the jade-green float of a Japanese fishnet
gleams in a tangle of seaweed
The tide withdraws and on the dampened sand
I see dim tracks of a girl's bare feet
curving and weaving awhile with the wave-line
then vanishing over the dunes
Dare I follow and come on her there
in some deep cleft of the dunes
nested down warm out of the sea wind
and the fog's raw breath?

DRAGONFLY

His wings refract the sun; their arabesques
are intricate as damascene; he rides
the tremors of the heat above the creek.
The dragonfly's all azure. With his mate
he couples in the air and sails elate
and unabashed before his smiling Lord.

FATAL AUTUMN

Sun on the leaves of my orchard
makes fiery flakes and coins of gold
Firs and redwoods raise vast green walls
to a sky more blue than sea
The air is still as that first instant

after death
No whisper of a breath shakes any leaf
and the valley at my feet
might be a landscape of lost Eden
seen through tears

THE HONEY WAGON MAN

"Gre't God! Yond' come de honey wagon man!"
You scented him and then he hove in sight
perched on his tank, a turkey buzzard on
a carcass. "Whoa!" he'd tell his whip-scarred mule,
hop off, unhook his buckets, head for a row
of privies and dig in. The bucketfuls
would slosh. Then back he'd climb. You'd hear his whip
whistle and crack until that half-dead mule
would pull. I used to wonder to myself
where does he go at night when kerosene
glints through the chinks of shot-gun alley shacks
and families sit down to supper? Who
would run to hug his spattered legs? What woman
fix him some greens with fatback and a pone?

JUST PEANUTS

Down in Georgia
one of the 13
original States of the Union
near the town of Americus
named after the man

America is named for
there is a farm
called Koinonia
meaning "community"

This Koinonia farm
has belonged to the people who work it
for 15 years
They have built it up
from just about nothing
until it can support
all 60 of them
Sixty people on 1,000 acres
which is pretty good going
if you know Georgia

These people are all religious
calling themselves Christians
like their neighbors
and some of them are even preachers
but because they took Negroes in
and treated them as brothers
their Christian neighbors
got some dynamite

With this dynamite
these Christian neighbors of theirs
white citizens of Americus
real 100 per cent Americans that is
blew up a lot of Koinonia's property
Then their Christian neighbors
shot into houses at night
where people were asleep
sprayed the kids' play yard
with machine gun bullets
cut fences and let the hogs out into the road
even shot a few hogs to teach them better

Mostly though
their Christian neighbors
worked it strictly legal
All insurance on the farm
was cancelled out

Nobody would buy
the stuff produced at Koinonia
the milk soured
the eggs went bad
5,000 good hens had to be trucked away
and sold for culls

You would think the people of Koinonia
would quit and all go away
but they haven't
and they don't
They work all day
stand watches all night
pray for their Christian neighbors
and all that really bothers them
is where to get seed peanuts
to plant their fields

They sent two women out and a little boy
aged nine
to try to buy peanuts up and down Georgia
One place a man cursed these women out
for "dirty niggerloving whores"
and yelled to raise a mob
but they escaped with their little boy
aged nine
and went on to another town
but when night came and they drove back home
they still had found no peanuts

A few ton of peanuts
is all they need
just peanuts . . .

MOLOCH

Butch Bardoli was just a ranch kid
a tow-head like yours or mine at seven
his pockets full of marbles
pieces of string
a tiny car or plane maybe
he'd got with a box top
Nothing extra about Butch
just the usual sort of small boy
and when the big cloud mushroomed
high into the cobalt desert sky
over the Reveille Mountains to the south
he stood in the yard with the six other children
who went to Twin Springs school
and watched with scared eyes

Now Butch Bardoli is dead of leukemia
or cancer of the bloodstream
It was just his hard luck to be born
there in that almost empty part of Nevada
where mountains thirty miles away
seem close enough to touch
and the dust devils whirl
on long hot summer days

As a great man said
"You can't make an omelet without breaking eggs"
a man named Nikolai Lenin
not George Washington or Thomas Jefferson or Abraham Lincoln
but we seem to have come over to his way of thinking
It does make a difference though
when it's an egg from your own nest
a beloved son perhaps
that gets broken for the omelet

Somewhere on the desert
a new cross stands
above a very short mound
and still the poisonous mushrooms climb the cobalt sky
over the Reveille range
but Butch Bardoli
sleeps on

INQUEST

A man lies dead today who yesterday
was working in his laboratory. He killed
himself. Killing himself he killed far more
besides. His research centered on the link
between twin scourges of mankind, cancer
and schizophrenia. This died with him.
Who knows what else? And all for what good end?
The man lies dead and cannot be subpoenaed
even by the Committee but awaits
that judgment which the Congressmen themselves
will some day stand to. He was accused of what?
Of nothing. If you prefer, of everything
that wild surmise can dream or sickest mind
invent. No fire in all the smoke? This much
perhaps, that in his youth he was deceived
by some who promised to redress world wrong.
(The Constitution left him free to make
his own mistakes.) Now, deep in a career
of dedicated service to mankind
he must confess, recant his early errors,
inform on friends whose guilt was no more real
than was his own. Or he must choose the way
of silence while men break him on the wheel
of public degradation, his sweating face
on television screens across the land,
a super-pillory where all may mock
and spit at him, his wife and children shamed
in every circle where they move, and then
the ultimate: his scientific work
halted, himself without a job or hope
of finding one, his family destitute . . .
And so he took the poison. What would you
have had him do, gentlemen of the Committee?

THE POLISHED CROSS

Inside the flawless chapel
for which the architect received a prize
Christ in low relief on granite
falls under a polished cross

Above the portal Mary mothers
a childish cluster while across
the terraced lawn within the offices
all gleaming glass the staff is gathered

"Embarrassing our topic for today
but we must squarely face it
The sin of sodomy is rife among
our boys and drastic measures are required

Above all vigilance . . . a constant watch
Make sure by peering underneath the door
two boys are never found to occupy
one toilet . . . Keep an eye upon the showers

Patrol the ballfield lest they hide
behind the backstop . . . Sneak beside the gym
and come upon them by the fire door
where weeds grow high and thick

Don't let a single pair of boys
get out of sight an instant
The kind we have here are abnormal
incorrigibly vicious

Let no new counselor imagine
he can accomplish anything
with kindness for the boys will think
it is the mark of weakness

Such men quit soon we find
or else we have to let them go
These boys are future criminals
and all they understand is force

Before we leave the subject
you might take down these names
of boys we have some reason to believe
corrupt the others . . . first Gonzales . . .

You'll find these Mexicans are all
inclined that way . . . Don't trust them . . .
Jackson next . . . Most Negroes are alike . . .
Sex mad and if they can't get girls

They'll take what they can get . . .
Antonelli . . . Italians are hot-blooded . . .
Smathers O'Rourke and Jankovich . . .
Degenerate stock in these three cases . . ."

Within the flawless chapel
for which the architect received a prize
a rough-hewn granite Christ
is nailed upon a polished cross

WE LOVE OUR CHILDREN

Every nice day
the children of San Francisco
walk through a tunnel under the Great Highway
that comes out on the beach
This tunnel is public property
which the paternal City has provided
for the safeguarding of its children
on their way to play in the sand

For months now I have been wondering
just how long it was going to take
the City Fathers of San Francisco
to get around to sponging off

the dirty words chalked all over the walls of this tunnel
and I had come to the conclusion
that nobody gave a damn
or at least nobody official

I now hear that to save the young from pollution
the San Francisco police have raided a bookshop
and arrested some people for selling to adults
literature containing the very same words in small print
that escape their attention when chalked large on public walls
where thousands of children pass by
All of which constrains me to comment
merde alors (Pardon my French)

FINISHING SCHOOL

A ten-foot fence that's topped with barbed wire strands
surrounds this finishing school. In star-marked cars
the girls are fetched by uniformed escorts.
Sad debutantes! Lovers you shall not lack.
Trapped female animals surpass the male
in viciousness. To frustrate vigilance
and woo each newcomer with arts practiced
on Sappho's isle is all their frenzy here.
The pool's a passion tank. About each pair
of furtive amorists fair mermaids sport
to screen their throes of love. Fine scenery
encompasses the school and visitors
exclaim. The picture windows when kicked out
by inmate heels make serviceable dirks,
stilettos, spears, from which psychologists
shrink back, and even deputies with guns.

AND EVER THE PYRES OF THE DEAD BURN THICK

Great Phoebus Apollo
unbend your silver bow
for mankind is weary of the slaughter
The proud the meek the foolish and the wise
the guilty and the innocent alike
die beneath your vengeful shafts
and never is there an end
to the hot blood smell

This woman now of Port Said
barefooted in her dress of rusty black
mounting a basket on her head
with cans of food raided from some sacked store
or flaming army dump
buys perhaps another week of life
for herself and orphaned brood
What is the crime of such as she
condemned to suffer so?

MARE NOSTRUM

Sea of ancient glory and modern misery
your waters are as stainless blue
as when your shores were unpolluted
by mankind
Liquid priestess of all times!
Vase of holy tears!
We call you ours
but rather we are yours
and when at last from Hellespont and Pharos
to where old Atlas groans beneath the world
only a vast necropolis confronts you
gazing vacant out to sea
you will mourn us with your surges
as a mother still rocks an infant
long after it has ceased to breathe

COMMERCIAL VEHICLES PROHIBITED

An Eden for the citizens who'd jeered
his dream McLaren conjured up from dunes.
We thread his pungent eucalyptic aisles
by tandem bicycle. Sun laced with fog
intoxicates, elixir of the air.
The castaways from Czernowicz and Czestochowa
stand watch around the sailing basin but
never a barque hauls round to their rescue.
"Welcome Dentists' Convention" succulents
declare. Fat dahlias droop. Lank bison too.
A languorous November, gold as May,
has tricked a rhododendron into bloom.
A shamefaced chauffeur walks a coiffeured poodle.
The pseudo-Grecian peristyle attracts
its quota of photographic devotees.
A maple with each scarlet leaf intact
flames on the waters where one idling swan
redeems a flock of ducks hustling for crusts.

San Francisco, 1957

HANGING GARDENS OF ZION

Improbably slime-rooted
the canyon sheer here
close to concave
Water drips two thousand feet through cracks
sustains
this wonder

Columbines yellow as sun-
washed altitudes
in shade perpetual
coral corollas
jack-priests in scarlet pulpits
spangling the steep

Secure
till it thunders and shakes them
down to perdition this very afternoon
A myriad leaves vote yea
Perpendicular gardens
you put me to shame

THE CONSERVATIVE ART

Typographia, ars artium omnium conservatrix.

The typographic skill of Dwiggins, late
an ornament of Boston, was enhanced,
his intimate letters reveal, when liquor cast
its spell over the hackneyed alphabet.
"Trim off the right-hand serif of the lower-
case N two-thousandths of an inch," he bade
the harried foundry-master. *Ars longa*,
Hippocrates averred, *vita brevis*. These pangs
ushered Electra in, lacklustre face
with Garamond for dam and Aldus sire,
now known from Norman's Woe to the Seal Rocks
on menus, posters, throw-aways. The great
typographer's ephemera, each scrawl,
doodle, comprise a precious trove for our
collection. Piously we catalog
matter minuscular while all about us
majuscule genius unperceived strides by.

SCULPTURES AT AN EXHIBITION

I. *Woman Under the Aspect of an Ash Tray*
Eyes show hauteur above lorgnetted nose
and lozenge lips. Cymbals with spouts figure
her paps, iconographic blasphemy.

Flared hips enclose a tray where men snuff out
their cigarettes or flick a token ash.
A wing-bolt aft denotes an orifice
that Phidias and Michelangelo
omitted from their female statuary.

II. Improved Centipede
Too many legs kept getting in his way.
Arthritis plagued him too. He traded all
his locomotor apparatus for
a wobbly wheel with broken spokes. Grandly
he rolls, a mounted nullipede. Two horns
sprout from his head and blare for right-of-way.

III. Maternity
Sawteeth have gashed her polished pedestal
suggesting menace of machine age. Prongs
exalt the whorl-grained pyx wherein gestate
enfolded gemini. Rich monstrance fit
to bear compare with pious artifacts,
aborted monster of contrivance—which?

IV. Eli, Eli, Lamma Sabacthani?
Gnarled driftwood adumbrates agony. We hear
the shout go down the wind. Elias? Who
was he? Caius, you crapped. Gimme them dice.

DAY OF STRANGE GODS

The gale-whipped grass lies flat along the dunes.
Pacific combers flash and boil in sun.
Here in their time an elder vatic breed,
"Inquiring, tireless, seeking what is yet unfound,"
came questioning the surf. Motels pre-empt
the shore now. Rocks, the habitat of seals,
are spied upon by tourists who let fall

from airborne gondolas their popcorn bags.
Along the lethal beachside freeway speed
the uncouth behemoths of the Baalish cult.
Four-eyed they glare and flaunt proctitic rumps
more hideous than the mandrill's. Frost was here
and Whitman too, beard streaming in the sea-wind:
"But where is what I started for so long ago,
And why is it yet unfound?" The poet Whitman
although a prophet profited but little
from the divining trade. A backward farmer,
Frost pitched his hay himself, dispensing with
the blessings of machinery. Tonight
at 8:04, astronomers predict,
the satellite will reappear, its arc
describing a trajectory fifteen
degrees above the crescent moon. "An age
of dark intent" the cryptic bard foretold
as he stood here in storm and hearkened to
the breakers' thunderous apocalypse.

THE MASTER OF YELLOW PLUM MOUNTAIN

The Master on the night wind scented death,
his own that sought him out. Within his cell
he sat serene awaiting the encounter
when hubbub arose from the scriptorium
shattering his contemplation of last things.
Contentious monks were sharpening a point
of doctrine. Such overweening disciples shamed
the master, he reflected, fanging the Way
of Truth with tigerish disputes. He could
foresee the tonsured brawlers around his bier
all snatching for his robe, the sacred garment
that Bodhi-Dharma wore from India
when he brought first the Buddha's luminous words
across Himalayas to the Middle Realm.

Foreknowledge made the Master flinch. He should
now pass the robe to whom he chose, as once
he had been vested by his predecessor
of blessed memory. But which of these
proud meretricious monks would not debase it?
In his extremity he thought of one
new to the brotherhood, scion of men
who, yoked with crusted buckets, at back doors
begged excrement of close-stools which they hawked
to peasants for enriching garden plots.
For all his forebears' noisome trade, the gate
was opened to this man, the monastery
being short of kitchen hands. The most abject
of scullions now he pounded husks from rice
to fatten nobler bellies than his own.
The Master rang and had him fetched. "Leave us!"
The startled messenger withdrew at this
command. The dying Master slowly rose,
removing from his back the Dharma robe
and spread it over deep-bowed, trembling shoulders.
"Go, lest your holy brethren and their knives
discover your investiture. Avoid
the roads and seek the mountain fastnesses.
Your heart will know the day you must return
to men and teach." That night the Master died.
Missing the robe, the enraged community
in arms sought to apprehend the fugitive
but he had vanished in the highest snows.

THE SIXTH GREAT PATRIARCH DECLINES

His crabbed brush indites: "Dread Lord! Your scroll's
superb calligraphy dazzles my eyes,
the eloquence of your minister my ears.
With tongue more silken than his gown
he bids me quit these rocky slopes for your

imperial palace. Could such inducements sway
my mind you'd gain another clown at court.
Your majesty mistakes his man. My bag
contains no magic tricks, no paper snakes
to affright the people or to make them clap.
The sutras are my only store, from them
I draw my poor powers, this robe the badge
of my superior emptiness. Husker
of rice was I. The Master for a sign
clothed me, the least of men, with Dharma. You,
I hear, are prone to heap old ivories,
patinaed bronze, pomegranite girls, eunuchs,
gold trinkets, jade, translucent porcelain.
Would you augment your hoard with my person,
another on the random list of self-
indulgences, a man clothed in the robe
once worn by Bodhi-Dharma, sealed thereby
both saint and sage, the wonder of the time?
Must I for strings of cash augur tea-cups,
discourse of voices heard upon the mountains,
pose mystical conundrums for myself
to crack like lichee nuts? Most august sire!
I must decline to be your holy fool.
Foolish I am in truth but keep my house
amongst my thousand monks where it is hid.
Besides the Dharma on my back wears thin
and ragged. In pity of my nakedness
the beggars at your gate might toss me coins."

ZION CANYON: EVENING

Named for a man, the Virgin river wears
an accidental grace. Her trout-rife reaches
darkle in the shadowed lees of colossi
whose thews of rosy stone she carved in moods
subliminal during her Maenad past.

What Byzantine basilica for all
its glittering glooms and fluted chrysoprase
but shrinks to bauble-scale measured by this
obdurate ecstasy of soaring rock?
Dour Mormon farm folk, first of our breed, fell
down on their knees before these high altars
that take the sunset molten on their planes.
The canyon fills with darkness but the light
lingers over Zion like an aureole.

VII

PHANTOM CITY
A Ghost Town Gallery, 1961

PAYS TO BE A HUNCHBACK IN LAS VEGAS

I knew a man in Phantom City
grew up twisted as a juniper
rooted in mountain rock
Peewee'd done most everything
a man could do in his condition
cooked for cow-hands on Nevada ranches
hung round the tables in Las Vegas
so gambling men could touch his hump for luck
and tip him silver dollars
(Pays to be a hunchback in Las Vegas)
He saved this dough
for which he'd swapped his pride
or what was left of it
(once in his life he'd hit Skid Row)
and bought his place in Phantom City

HIGH CLASS JUNQUE he advertised
playing the tourists
Might as well put SMALL POX on his sign
as WORKS OF ART
Here in a shop not big enough
to pitch a pup-tent in
all camouflaged with odds and ends
fat ladies throned on midget toilet bowls
plastic skeletons and spooks
mass-produced for ghost-town tourist traps
Peewee hung his paintings

Mostly Christs
as I remember
strange Christs that smiled
beneath their crowns of thorns
Doc bought one for his Rock Shop
and swore it wept real tears
still smiling
and worked a miracle on a customer
but Doc had been

in booby-hatches off and on
so maybe not

Still there they were
those Christs
nobody'd buy outside of Doc
though sometimes Peewee would
get in a show at Santa Fe
with a western landscape or a costumed Indian
somebody'd buy because
the thing had passed a jury
That's the public for you

This Peewee had his faults
So far as anyone could tell
Peewee never took a bath
maybe because he had no tub or running water
upstairs in that ruin where he lived
What's more old Peewee mooched
drinks at the Rio Grande Bar off those flush
construction men in helmets from the dam
big-hearted guys
or was it only like taking out insurance?
Where they were drilling on the canyon wall
it was a thousand feet straight down
Up at the bar I saw their arms around his hump

THE FEUD

People feuded more
in Phantom City
than any place I ever was
Always picking at each other
got to be a habit with them

Take Miss Irma Weed and Judge Tim Feeney
Religion could have been behind it
Irma being Eastern Star

a lady Mason like
while Tim was Grand Knight of Columbus
Old-timers said the two despised each other
far back as grade school fifty years before
and had been faithful haters
ever since

More than likely Irma took offense
at the business Tim's old man was in
"Feeney's Elite Hotel" he called it
Pay-day night he really made it big
and rented every bed two dozen times
(Mike Feeney picked his hookers for endurance)
and Tim (before he got elected judge)
dealing blackjack in the parlor

The story goes that Irma's fellow had a steady
named Carmencita
in Room 13 at Feeney's
and this you hardly could expect her to forgive
Irma being what you call
a real good Christian

Well here they were
the Judge and Irma
gray-headed
but still battling it out
and all of Phantom City lining up
on one side or the other
because there wasn't any middle
They don't allow neutrality in that town

So at last we got the celebrated case
Weed vs Feeney
unique in the annals of so-called jurisprudence
contesting the ownership of two worthless pictures
a leopard and a grizzly bear
in frames with bars in front like cages
that used to hang in Feeney's lobby
where the boys would wait their turns
to go upstairs on pay-day night

The Judge had lent the pictures out
to the town Improvement Club

which hung them in an empty store front
fixed up for atmosphere with dummies
old prospector with his burro
fancy woman showing off her leg
whiskerinos playing stud
just fakery to catch the tourist's eye
and make him park to gawk
and maybe spend a buck or two
for ghost-town curios

The store front glass was broken
and anybody with a mind to
could have trucked the whole sideshow away
If anything in that window was worth stealing
it sure God would have disappeared in Phantom City

Now the Judge had two old uncles
bad characters the both of them
inmates at the County Home
who came to Phantom City on a jag intending
to strike the Judge up like they had his dad lifelong
for guzzling money
The Judge gave them the bounce unkinsmanlike
so on they staggered
plotting their revenge
to Irma's Spooktown Sandwich Shoppe

The pictures of the leopard and the grizzly bear
Tim's uncles swore to Irma
were theirs by rights
and back in 1917 had hung in their saloon
the Scorpion
but their whoremaster of a brother Mike
father to that holy bastard Tim
had swiped the pictures to beautify his cat-house
while the two of them were overseas in 1918
saving civilization from the Huns
(That pair had never worn a uniform
but loafed in shipyards through the war)

Irma paid the two old rips
a five-spot for the pictures
and off they sprinted to the Silver Spur Saloon

while Irma spread the tidings
that the leopard and the grizzly now were hers
by right of purchase from the lawful owners
As a public service to the town
Irma announced
she'd leave the pictures in the store front
but she wanted everyone to know
they were her property

When the news reached Tim
he threw a fit
and hired a six foot seven kid named Elihu
(on probation from his court)
to steal them from the broken window
but Irma kept a watch and spotted Elihu
fleeing from the scene of crime
with a picture under each long arm

Indictments next were served
on Elihu and on the Judge
ex parte Irma Weed
for co-conspiracy to commit grand theft
The Judge had to vacate the bench
and on his case presided
the lady judge from Avalanche
Irma's sister in the Eastern Star

The lady judge came into court
with verdict all typed in advance
(She was Republican plus Eastern Star
No popish Democrat stood a chance with her)
Tim's uncles had their day
getting square with their dead brother Mike
He'd set them up in business once
staked them to their saloon
and they had failed
God damn him!

No one felt like laughing
when court adjourned that day
though up to then
some of us had
Tim hung the leopard and the grizzly back

among the dummies in the fake display
and there they'll hang I guess
till the Lord smites Phantom City flat

Irma queened it for a week or two
Then something new came up
and people forgot about her famous victory
Tim Feeney though
the Judge
he never did forget it
He just pined away to nothing
Cancer the doctor said it was
eating out his insides
but that wasn't all
Shriveled to a skeleton
a crucifix above his bed
Tim lay there babbling
"That bigoted old baggy!
That bitch Irma Weed!
I'll appeal the case!
I'll git them pitchers yet!"

HOMBRE DE DIOS

Padre Tomás Echeverría
was a handy man to have around
the Anglos said who ran the town
of Phantom City
Born in Spain himself
the Padre had that fine Castilian pride
and looked down on the mixed-blood
Mexicans of his flock
He threatened with the flames of hell
parishioners of his who joined a labor union
for that was Communism in his book

and when a García or a Gómez
went snuffing after some young Anglo bitch
Padre teamed up with the Masons and the Eastern Star
to save the purity of the race
white that is

They foxed the Padre once though
when Mrs Farnum's daughter Lou
by I forget which of her marriages
eloped with Juan Romero
Seems one of her mother's drinking buddies
had put Lou up the stack at age 16
but wouldn't do the gentlemanly thing
and pay for an abortion
Juan took pity on the girl
He'd loved her hopelessly before
He let her have her baby and gave his name to it
but Mrs Farnum wouldn't let him carry it to church
for Padre to baptize
A Romero unbaptized!
The scandal of it like to broke old Padre's heart

The Padre had his points
He was the best mechanic in New Mexico
and could make anything on four wheels
get up and git
Padre had what he called his ranch
a beat-up shack out past the tailings dump
where he fed homeless cats
and where he kept relaxing literature
he didn't want the bishop on his pop-in pastoral calls
to catch a sight of
Padre played a mean piano too
Summer evenings down beneath the church
where he lived all alone
you'd often hear the tinkling of his tunes
the kind they used to dance to
in sporting-houses when the town was young

A TOLERANT WOMAN

Bud Hildreth married a Mexican girl
Dolores Maldonado
his secretary in the office at the mine
They said he did it to get even with his sweetheart
Juney Brattigan who ran off with an army captain
The mine shut down but Bud was kept
as custodian of company property
Dolores too stayed on the payroll
and went on doing Bud's work for him
Elected President of the Phantom City Improvement Club
Bud got the company to donate them a building
and opened up a reptile museum for the tourists
He fixed himself a layout on the second floor
supposed to be the headquarters for the club
but soon Bud's old sweetheart Juney
made it hers
She'd come back from army life divorced
and with the taste of army wives for booze
She and Bud put in a kitchen and a private bar
with TV and a nice big couch
but to keep things all respectable
Bud's wife Dolores
had dinner with them in their hide-away
every Sunday
which people said was pretty tolerant of Juney
Dolores being Mexican

CREATION UNLIMITED

They closed the silver mine in '48
and most of Phantom City moved away
Things were pretty dead round town
till word got out

and artists started coming in
to find themselves cheap quarters
I guess they were no worse than natives
but they sure were different

The first artist to come
rented himself a store for five a month
and advertised
CREATION UNLIMITED
in big block letters all across the front
His way of working was to set
some cans of house paint round the floor
with sticks in them
and drip paint off the sticks onto
wallpaper that he stripped
from empty houses

It doesn't matter what the guy was named
He took an interest in the children hanging round
his studio because they hadn't anything else to do
The company had drained the swimming pool
blocked off the tennis courts and baseball field
and closed the people's clubhouse down
Soon all the kids in town were creating masterpieces
by dripping paint off sticks
but then the whisper got around
the guy was propositioning the boys

It might have been the truth
and just as easily might not
Suspicion was enough
Whoever asked for proof
must be that way himself
The committee dumped the guy
way off the highway in the blazing desert
Nobody has reported finding bones out there
so maybe he made it back to civilization
if that's the word

OLD MRS FINCH AND THE BIBLE SALESMAN

Widowed but she kept her head up
every day no matter what
She'd been around that old girl
and knew the world
Her husband Dr Finch had been an anthropologist
and she had learned plenty from him
She came to Phantom City from the reservation
when he died
and fixed an old place up
she'd gotten for a bargain
She was damned she said if she would live
with any of her married sons back East
and spar for status with another female
Like I say
she knew some anthropology
Just the same she missed her boys
Mrs Finch
so when that Bible salesman came around
Herb Whipple was his name
and said he'd like to settle down
she let him have the apartment in her basement
He was a nice-appearing kid
and appreciated Mrs Finch's view
Wasn't long till he was spending evenings on her porch
and she was cooking for him
as well as paying all his bills
When time came for her to go to bed
the Bible salesman strolled on down to the Silver Spur
and slopped up beers till the barkeep locked the doors
This Whipple was 25 and Mrs Finch was over 70
but Phantom City had them lovers
in no time
People couldn't seem to figure
how a woman with her sons grown up and gone
might try to find some boy to substitute
and play the sucker for him
the same as for her own
right gladly
and with her eyes wide open

AMPUTEE

Miles Randall lost an arm in Spain
fighting in the Brigade
but something else was amputated deep inside
when he came home and found himself
blacklisted for his heroism
He stopped believing in a thing
himself included
He'd stay dead drunk for months on end
not caring where he slept
on floors or any place he passed out
not caring where his latest wife slept either
Then he'd come to one day and write a storm
of stories laid in Phantom City's romantic past
He'd sell a few
(He had a following in pulps)
and off he'd go on another drunk
Miles would be blind in the Rio Grande Bar
while his wife was slopped in the Silver Spur
and the Mexicans saw that their kid didn't starve

THE END OF A GRAVE ROBBER

Elrod Logan worked at contracting
when times were good round Phantom City
He and his old lady had a pastime
legal when they started years ago
of digging up the graves in cliff-house ruins
where Pueblo Indians used to live
six and eight hundred years ago
They found a lot of pots
with human bones in some of them
and had themselves a houseful
when the government clamped down
and sent a ranger out to threaten people

who dug up Indian ruins
they'd go to jail unless they quit

Elrod's old lady died about that time
and he who'd always been a sober man
went on a four-year drunk
He wrecked a good hotel he owned
just to get the plumbing out
to sell for whiskey
The pots he and his wife had dug were sold off
one by one for bust-head
He brought a pair of bleary-eyed old biddies home
he'd picked up in an Albuquerque bar
and turned the place his wife had fixed so nice
with Navaho rugs and Spanish furniture
into an old folks' whorehouse
You could hear them raising hell at night
and Elrod all of eighty
He ran into another car while driving drunk
and had his license pulled for ninety days
He drove drunk again before a week went by
and had his license pulled for good
That finished him
He sold his house and went to live
in Denver with a son of his
Two months later he was dead
We never heard what of
but most of Phantom City thought
those Indians whose graves he robbed
had taken care of Elrod in their way

THE COLONEL'S ARTHRITIS

Being just an artist was too rough
he found
too little in it for a man
who liked to eat on schedule
so he decided all that self-expression

could wait a while
and grabbed himself a paying job
He rode the cushions all his life
curator in museums
even rear echelon colonel in the army
and then retired to Phantom City
with pensions from all over
to nurse arthritis
and just paint
You know
the pictures that he did
had arthritis too
and pretty soon
the Colonel was running everything again
President of the Artists' League and such

DESERT HOLY MAN

Old Charley Garber delivered ice
to all the whorehouses in Spokane
when he was young
He had to admit the broads were good to him
but what a start in life
for a mystical philosopher
a yogi and a vegetarian

Charley did a Navy hitch
worked cargo in Seattle
helped build the San Francisco bridges
and moved machinery in L.A.
where he got mixed up with yoga
occult sciences and carrot juice

When his wife passed on
Charley came to Phantom City with his mind made up
to live the life of spiritual essence
which he mostly did

except for playing poker with the firemen now and then
He was Chief and drove the fire engine
with a helmet on his long white flying hair
and his Viking whiskers blowing

Charley had a clunker truck
rigged up for desert prospecting
Weeks at a time he'd disappear
collecting rocks to cut and burnish
His shack was full of saws and buffing tools
blocks of rainbow agate jasper and onyx
pure turquoise chunks
blue crystal azurite and velvet malachite

Charley could work silver like a Navaho
belt buckles set with flashing stones
heavy necklaces and bracelets
rings with turquoise nuggets
but Charley was no salesman
He charged you what
he thought you could afford to pay
and loaned his money out
to every panhandler
He even set Kid Anaconda up in business
to be his competitor in town!

People thought old Charley was an easy mark
and took advantage of him
but Doc Odell went too far once
and said to some guys in the Silver Spur
as Charley walked in for a beer
"Here comes that old vegetarian son of a bitch"
Doc hit the floor so hard he bounced
Old Charley spit on his hands
and stood the drinks around

TERROR OF THE WEST

Gorilla for the copper bosses in Montana
Kid Anaconda claimed he used to be
He had the build for it beneath a ton of lard
and swaggered round Phantom City like he owned it
To hear him tell
he'd been the terror of the West
and would double up beer bottle caps
between his finger and his thumb to settle any doubts

When he was special deputy on duty
one Saturday night
some hoodlums from El Paso
got in a free for all outside the Rio Grande Bar
kicking in faces with their cowboy heels
Kid Anaconda didn't leave his pinball game inside
Said his authority was limited
just to protecting property
and seeing kids obeyed the curfew
He didn't want to run the risk
of someone suing him for false arrest

Kid Anaconda loved most of all to fight with women
He rented half of Gertie Quirk's Old Western Beanery
when Old Man Garber staked him to a stock of rocks
He never did much business
but ran a non-stop poker game in his side
till Gertie Quirk tipped off the Sheriff
Just a curtain hung between
and when her tourist customers
heard all that poker cussing with their meals
it got to be
a little bit too western for them

Kid Anaconda ate from then on at the Chinaman's
and persuaded Old Man Garber to do the same
claiming that Gertie was a money-grubbing slut
who charged a nickel more for pie
and cut the slices smaller
than anyone in Yucca county

Even Old Man Garber got fed up with him at last
and told how Kid Anaconda'd lived for years on mama
and when she died
married a beauty operator with a house and income
and camped on her
until she threw him out
Kid Anaconda claimed
his wife had made him sign his property over to her
(his share in hers that is)
$60,000 worth
and then asked for a divorce

"I let her keep the God damn property" he'd say
"If she was that big of a bitch
I wouldn't stoop to argue with the whore
but" (Here he'd flex his thick fingers up
and shake those gorilla arms of his)
"I could of killed her with these two hands"

A ROPE AND TYING TEAM

Sue and old Bob Turlock came to Phantom City
and bought the Silver Spur Saloon
A model pair
they didn't either of them take a drink or even smoke
Old Bob had more than thirty years on Sue
but he looked vigorous at 78
Fought lightweight in the ring when he was young
and he and Sue had been a famous rope and tying team
at rodeos all over
Sue still dressed the part
pearl button shirts
tight western pants and cowboy boots
but prim and prissy!
Except for that outfit she wore
she could have been a schoolma'am sipping pop
among the drunks rough-housing in the Silver Spur

Then that construction crew moved into town
to work on the Downriver dam
Evenings they'd hang around
when Sue was tending bar
One night she wasn't there
and neither was the usual crew
till near closing time she blasted in
with her construction gang in tow
drunker than anybody ever saw a woman
and started cussing out old Bob
That prissy Sue had a command of dirty language
to make an out-house poet jealous
Old Bob just took her filth
till Sue began to heave expensive bottles at him
full of rum and whiskey off his shelves
All he did was put her out right gently
and close the bar and go to bed

Not Sue though
For a solid week she roared
and frolicked with her construction men
beat on their doors at 3 AM
screaming to be let in
To get some rest these guys
had to call in the Sheriff
and have her put away for thirty days
in the county jail as a D & D

She came back sober to old Bob
and just like nothing had ever happened
he took her in
Appears she was the daughter of a pard of Bob's
and he'd known her from a baby
helped bring her up
and when she turned to booze and men
pulled her through a hundred scrapes
even went on the wagon with her
and married her to help her kick the habit

All serene at the Silver Spur
for a couple of months
Sue prissed around
same as before

and made you halfway think
you must have dreamed the things she'd done
till one day someone kiddingly asked her
to join him in a beer and that was it
She did

Sue moved Tony López and his brother Jesús in with her
and threw her husband out of his own trailer
She filed for a divorce on grounds of old Bob's cruelty
and told the world she was going to marry Tony
who'd walked out on his wife and seven hungry kids
Bob agreed to let Sue have the trailer and the Cadillac
but when he went down in his rattletrap truck
to get his saddle and some other gear of his
Tony and his brother Jesús jumped him
and when they had him down
kicked in all his ribs
while Sue kept hopping up and down
just begging them to kill him

Tony López and his brother Jesús blew town that night
and Phantom City never saw the two of them again
Old Bob came out of the hospital
(They couldn't keep him there)
taped up like a mummy
He asked Kid Anaconda from next door
to keep bar for him
and took off somewhere
A while after old Bob had left
Kid Anaconda thought to look
in that drawer underneath the bar where Bob
stowed away the 45
The gun was gone
Kid Anaconda weighs close to 300 pounds
and isn't what you'd call a fast man usually
but this time he moved

Kid Anaconda and the Sheriff
pulled up to where Sue's trailer was
beneath some cottonwoods down by the river
Busting in they found
Bob with that 45 up to her head and cocked
For fifty minutes by the clock

Sue claimed and she was the one to know
he'd held that automatic's muzzle to her temple
while he reviewed for her
how many varieties of bitch she'd been all of her life
and Bob wasn't a talkative man
When he got through the narrative he promised her
he'd kill her
and afterwards himself
Good thing the old man's memory held out

AND THE LORD TAKETH AWAY

Mario Martínez cut people's hair
back when there were enough of them in Phantom City
to support a barber shop
Between customers he studied up the Bible
and decided that his people ought to have
a Spanish Bible church in town
Down on a rise beside the dump
he built his church himself
from old blasting powder boxes
scrap boards and salvage
It even had a sort of steeple
and Mario held services
although the Padre preached against him
and tried to run him out of town
But when the mine shut down
so did the barber shop
and after that the Bible church
Mario had built it piece by piece
and now he watched his jobless people
pull it down again the way he built it
piece by piece to feed their kitchen stoves
If he minded
he wasn't letting on

VIII

POEMS
1961–1974

HOMAGE TO A SUBVERSIVE
For H. D. T. 1817–1862

Soon, Henry David, wind will fill the land
saluting your centenary. Do you
suppose that alma mater's orators
at her memorial solemnities
will quote: "What branches of learning did you
find offered while at Harvard, Mr. Thoreau?"
"All of the branches and none of the roots."
And will Concord's divines in eulogies
of you dwell on the public scandal of
your unchurched life and unrepentant end?
"It's time to make your peace with God, Henry!"
"I'm not aware," the long-faced death-watch heard
you quip, "that God and I have ever quarreled."

The pietists who con your works by rote
forswear you and themselves with servile oaths
to placate golfing clerics, bawds of the press,
snoopers, war-hawks, kept Congressmen. Silent
they stand while lying leaders make our name
odious to men, shield tyrants with our might,
huckster new-packaged servitude for freedom,
and dub the peoples' butchers "democrats."
The coffle of pampered house-slaves will dare hymn
you dead. Come back! They'll turn you in. "How should
a man behave toward this government
today? I answer, that he cannot without
disgrace associate himself with it."

WISDOM OF THE ABBOT MACARIUS I

Said he: "I can no longer sanction
    any war for any purpose
        under God's sun or stars"
And they put him in chains

Said he: "I can no longer sanction
    any war for any purpose
        under God's sun or stars"
And they showed him the scaffold

Said he: "I can no longer sanction
    any war for any purpose
        under God's sun or stars"
And they laid his head on the block

Said he: "I can no longer sanction
    any war for any purpose
        under God's sun or stars"
And the ax fell

Whereupon the multitude fell silent
    thinking
        well
He could be right

ENGAGEMENT AT THE SALT FORK

Like tumbleweeds before the wind we moved
across the continent's huge heedless face.
Fat sheriffs' radios kept hot with news
of our invasion. Squad-cars tailed the walk.
Blasts born on Yukon tundras knifed us through
and buffeted our sign: *Man Will End War
Or War Will End Man.* Handful that we were,
armed men patrolled us, secret agents sped
ahead to warn the elevator towns.

Christians heard now that if they harbored us
and let us spread our sleeping-bags on floors
of Sunday schools, religion would be lost.
Whoever opened up his door to us
was spotted by a telephoto lens,
proclaimed suspect, anathema to all
right-thinking patriots. As if we were
the ghosts of banished Cherokees come back,
the guilty Strip shook in its cowboy boots.
We camped one night beside the Salt Fork, near
a town through which they'd hustled us with guns
and imprecations lest ideas start
an epidemic there. Our campfire lit,
potatoes boiling and someone's guitar
strumming *Down by the Riverside,* people
began to drift in from the country round.
Skylarking students with a bugle, torches,
burlesquing us with signs: *Workers Arise!*
You Have Nothing to Lose but Your Thirst! Drink Beer!
Good kids they proved to be and soon knocked off
the clowning. Faces in the firelight grew
into hundreds, boys with their dates, big-hats
from nearby ranches, preachers whose wives had brought
us popcorn, apples. A dozen arguments
swirled into being as good-humoredly
they challenged us to win their minds with fact
and logic. Raw though the night, shirt-sleeved they stood
and battled with us till they came to see
the meaning of our walk. Some would have joined
had we sought that. One horse-breeder, Stetsoned
and powerful of frame, told of campaigns
he'd fought in Italy. Fondling his son,
a lad of eight, he blessed our walk for peace.
"Each war *we* fight, *they* promise is the last,"
he said, "and here they go ag'in. This boy
is one they ain't a-goin' to git, by God!"
Long after midnight it was when the last
of them went home. I could not sleep for pride
in these my people, still square-shooters, still
ready to tote fair with the other man.
I could not sleep for sadness too, to think
how these great hearts are gulled with lies.
God help the liars when my people wake!

THE SEED OF FIRE
For Highlander Folk School

The celluloid is old. It snaps and must
be spliced. The worn-out sound-track garbles words.
But here they are, the marching union men,
the girls with banners. Pitiful! A torrent
of mountain water plunging from the rocks
to lose itself downstream in stagnant sloughs,
mud-clogged meanderings and stinking pools.
The nation rots. What we were once looks out
of this old film with shining eyes. Where did
we miss our way? New men rise up with skins
dark-hued to take the vanguard place of those
grown compromised and well content to rake
fat winnings from the gamble of death. Dark too
those women who indomitably face
plantation lords and teach sea-island folk,
disfranchised all their voiceless lives, to stand
and vote. Here is the continuity,
the precious seed of fire in these sad ashes.

GONE

If you're looking for him here you might
as well give up. I doubt if he'll be back.
That sermon on our Christian duty to
pay tax for bombs was more than even he
could take. Maybe he's gone to Tennessee.
You've heard of how those Negroes registered
to vote and how their landlords threw them off
their farms and how the Negroes pitched a camp
and called it Freedom City. That's the kind
of place you're apt to find him. Jailed maybe

for bringing food and blankets in like that
preacher McCrackin all the elders and
high priests are out to get. Might even be
he ran the block to Cuba. Can't stop him
once he makes up his mind to see things for
himself. Could be he's building them a school
or housing for the folks of the *bohíos*.
That wouldn't be a trade he'd need to learn.

UNDESIRABLES

I lift my lamp beside the golden door
    Emma Lazarus. Inscription for the Statue of Liberty

The lifted lamp is guttering, near spent
its fuel. Double-barred the golden door
which, when it opens, opens on a chain.
Where throngs poured through, police interrogate
each refugee, admitting but the few
who pass security and kiss the Book.
Carl Schurz would be excluded with his staunch
compatriots of Eighteen Forty-Eight
whose rebel blood caused liberty to grow
in their adopted land. Could Juárez get
a visa from the State Department? Would
the FBI clear Dvořák, known to be
in sympathies an anti-monarchist?
(Deport the New World Symphony!) Martí,
the Cuban foe of imperialism? Lorca,
the anti-fascist poet? These men were all
subversive as in earlier times Tom Paine,
Pulaski, Lafayette. The authorities
would surely bar such undesirables.

AZTEC FIGURINE

"Ray-*hee*-nah!"
            "Ya voy, señora!"
                          All day on
the double with her mop and pail, huaraches
tattooing tile, small Aztec figurine
with no more bust or hip-span than a *chica*
at first communion. Three Caesareans
to pry her babies out. Her man is down
with ulcers. Even when he works he drinks
his little money up and lives with some
puta. Regina's shanty's built from cans
and crates high up the *Montuoso*. That's
the *barrio* without a water tap
for fifteen thousand people. Trucks come in
and sell it by the litre. There's a queue
at every out-house. Most just use a pot
and throw it in the street. Planes bomb the place
with DDT. At six Regina locks
her children in and goes to work. It's dark
when she gets home. She lights a candle then
beneath two pictures on the wall, Our Lady
of Guadalupe and by her side Fidel.

DON GREGORIO FROM OMAHA

Their constitution says we can't own land.
Mordida to officials, partnerships
with native stooges and you've got it made.
Greg Watkins picked an hacienda up
dirt cheap. He made his peons call him "Don
Gregorio" and take sombreros off
when he rode by like some old *hacendado*.
Big Em was "Doña Manuela" to all

her barefoot servants. Jesus, what a deal!
Then that *ejido* trouble started. Reds,
Greg called them, squatted on his property,
claimed they were starving so they had a right
to plow his best horse pastures up for corn.
Greg's got to buy a greaseball general
to run the buggers off with bayonets.

BESTRIDE THE NARROW WORLD

Why, man, he doth bestride the narrow world
Like a Colossus, and we petty men
Walk under his huge legs and peep about
To find ourselves dishonourable graves.
                    JULIUS CAESAR, I, ii

We dangled them upon the edge a week
letting them savor death and then reprieved
them from their jeopardy a space. The style
is new. The abominations of his war
moved Lincoln to unmanly tears. Perhaps
he pondered Scripture overmuch. We too
bring God into our speeches. Fustian
we spout as well to cloak our naked sword
in words of righteous tone. Small matter if
the skeptical are unconvinced. We have
the countervailing force to make them cringe.
No power makes us stoop to parley. Proud
as pterodactyls in their prime are we,
mighty as mammoths whose unrivaled thews
the tundra binds in ice perpetual.

CONFORMITY MEANS DEATH
For Bertrand Russell

Our time's true saint he is, whose fealty
transcends the bounds of nation, tribe and clan,
embracing all who inhabit earth and their
inheritors. The voice we hear is more
than his. Through him the unborn of our loins
plead that we interpose our bodies now
between them and the Juggernaut we've built.
"Conformity means death!" No rhetoric
but starkest truth he speaks. Throw road blocks up
to Armageddon with your flesh. Besiege
the supine parliaments which veto peace
and cast their purchased votes for war. Let them
not sleep for your outcry. Fast unto death
if need be. Nail your picket signs upon
the doors of churches that usurp the cross
and grossly mock the One they feign to serve.
(He is not mocked but bides His awful time.)
Then rise! "Protest alone gives hope of life!"

A VETERAN'S DAY OF RECOLLECTION

We'd liberated Naples and the Wops
had come aboard to work cargo. This starving
Spik slipped a can of rations underneath
his lousy rags. We drilled him. At Marseilles
we mowed a stevedore down for pilfering
some Spam. The Battle of the Bulge was on,
V-bombs had knocked out Antwerp but the God
damned Frogs struck every ship of ours in port.
P-40's shot up Palermo for the hell
of it. Pinpoint objectives? Tenements!

Krauts wrecked Le Havre's docks and blew. The town
was open. Flying Fortresses blasted
it flat and left some thirty-thousand dead
allies of ours. Christ, how those ruins stank!
GI's in Germany went "one to shoot
and three to loot." We always gave
a Hershey to the frauleins that we ganged.

A MEDITATION ON THE FLAG

1862–1962

Framed in her attic window in Frederick town,
shaking her banner out at dour Stonewall,
bidding him *Shoot, if you must, this old gray head,*
But spare your country's flag, Dame Barbara
gave Whittier his noblest theme. Her myth
enshrines a symbol sacred to us once
though worse defiled now than by rebel shot.
Green hills of Maryland wall Frederick
as then but chimneys dwarf the "clustered spires."
Old Glory floats above a devilish hive
where secretly we manufacture toxins
so potent that an ounce could wipe out millions.
Here traitor scientists impregnate hordes
of bugs with virulent bacteria
so each mosquito, fly, louse, tick, and flea
carries a war-head of bubonic plague,
typhus, the bloody flux, cholera, anthrax,
or yellow-jack. Here pathogens are bred
to blight the healthy crops and famish nations.
Here too in squat retorts, alembics, vats
they brew, distill and synthesize the fumes
to drive whole cities mad, strike children blind
and slay in paroxysmal agonies
windrows of innocents for others' deeds.

What crime in all man's ghastly history
can stand with this prepared in Frederick
beneath the poet's "symbol of light and law"?
Haul down the stars and stripes! Run up the flag
we really serve—black, with the skull and bones!

FREE WORLD NOTES

I
Lowdown white sonofabitch
comin in here and stirrin up our niggers to vote
lemme at him with this here blackjack
the cops done turned their backs

II
I find you guilty Brenda Travis age 16
of an aggravatin breach of the public peace
for sittin down at the counter
of the bus station cafe
and I therefore sentence you
to one year's imprisonment
in the colored females' reformatory

III
We the coroner's jury bein duly sworn
do find that State Rep'sentative Hurst
did whip Herbert Lee a nigra boy age 52
right smart over the head with the butt of his pistol
and did also fire a 45-caliber projectile
into the nigra's intercranial cavity
such bein the proximate cause of said Herbert's demise
and we do further find and pronounce
this act to have been justifiable homicide
the nigra boy havin provoked the Rep'sentative
unwarrantably
by insistin that he be registered on the book
and permitted to vote like a citizen

YOURS IN THE BONDS

Brother, your appeal's at hand. Our house
through long neglect decays. We must infuse
at once and massively the cash to heal
time's ravages, perpetuate the breed
we're noted for, oarsmen and athletes of
the bottle, clean-cut types whose fathers sit
on the Exchange. If we decline to act
the university will seize our house,
restore and lease it back to us at cost
of cherished principle. We might be forced
to take a Jew, Negro, or Indian.
Must we then foot the bill? A bitter choice!
Fat though our winnings from portfolios
and corporations we manipulate,
it's most repugnant to our principles
to make donations not deductible.
We joined our dearly beloved fraternity
to turn a profit, not incur a loss.
It was our lofty object to latch on
to lads who counted in the world, scions
of Munsingwear or Listerine or U.
S. Steel. The secret grip, the ritual
and all that garbage went along, quaint old
survivals from an age of squares who took
this jovial fraternal bit for real.
In 1853 Grandfather joined
at Williams, then a hick establishment.
The bumpkin "Prex" sat on a log and you
upon the other end and that, they claimed,
was education. Lots of good it did
Grandfather, all his wasted life a parson
who shared his pittance with the poor. When Father
matriculated at Cornell, Ezra's
egalitarian injunctions still
prevailed. A loutish school. The chapter house
was just a clapboard shack on Lake Street hill.
Later a turreted mansion was acquired
to accommodate a band increasingly
elite. In martial Teddy's times it burned
and boys were trapped. The brothers braved the flames

in vain attempts at rescue. They too died.
A note on White House stationery bears
high witness to their heroism. I
would not detract nor could I add a word.
Suffice it that the house burned down with loss
of life deplored by all. Insurance was
in force, the Lord be praised. Alumni dug
another bundle up and reared the pile
where I, a double legacy, was pledged,
initiated, taught to swill and wench.
Here I absorbed contempt for scholarship,
bitch goddess worship and a fake mythos
that made me dream myself superior
to all beyond the pale of our sweeping
greensward. Tricked out in coonskin coats and suits
from Brooks, we saw the world as our private
demesne to plunder rightfully while our
inferiors stood helplessly aside.
You ask me, brother, for my honest views.
My voice is for abandoning this relic
or willing it to the authorities to do
with as they wish. The brotherhood we preached
and practiced was a fraud. Not love but hate
united us—the vilest kind that hates
a man because his name or skin is wrong,
oblivious to what at heart he is.

"CHAINEY"

The field boss claimed his privilege. Her knife
quenched all his lust for black girls. She got life
in the Big Rock and swung a chain-gang pick
a quarter century before she broke.
To save her keep they kicked her out, paroled.
Root, hog, or die! Thereafter she despoiled

our garbage cans of what our pampered pets
repudiated. We capering white brats
dogged her around, mocking that tethered gait.
She shambled rolling-eyed down every street
in Birmingham, mumbling of "Jedgment." All
our minds were shackled by her chain and ball.

A DIXIE HERO

Ole Raymon seed this black boy comin long
the walk an didn' lahk his looks so he
retch down an grab a gre't big rock an stove
damn nigguh's head in faw him. Nevah seed
so comical a thang sence Ah been bawn.
Ole Raymon bust a hole big as a half
a dollah spang in his fo'head. Cain't kill
no nigguh thataway. They skulls is bone
clean th'oo. Well, Raymon got th'owed outa school.
Shit, not faw that. He cussed the principal.

TO LIVE AND DIE IN DIXIE

I

Our gang
laid for the kids from niggertown
We'd whoop from ambush chunking flints
and see pale soles
of black feet scampering
patched overalls and floursack pinafores
pigtails with little bows

flying on the breeze
More fun than birds
to chunk at
Birds
were too hard to hit

II

Old Maggie's sweat would drip and sizzle
on that cast iron range she stoked
but she was grinding at the handle
of our great big ice cream freezer
that day she had her stroke
It put a damper on my mother's luncheon
All the ladies in their picture hats and organdies
hushed up until the ambulance took Maggie off
but soon I heard
their shrieks of laughter
like the bird-house at the zoo
while they spooned in
their fresh peach cream

III

Asparagus fresh from the garden
my dad insisted
went best on breakfast toast with melted butter
so Rob was on the job by six
He used to wake me whistling blues
and whistled them all day till plumb
black dark when he got off
Times Mother was away
he'd play piano for me
real barrelhouse
(I liked it better than our pianola classics)
and clog on the hardwood floor
Rob quit us once to paper houses on his own
but white men came at night and sloshed
paint all over his fresh-papered walls
took the spark plugs out of his Model T truck
poured sand into the cylinders
then screwed the plugs back in
so when Rob cranked it up next day
he wrecked the motor
He came back to work for us

but I can't seem to remember
him whistling much again

IV

Black convicts in their stripes and shackles
were grading our schoolyard
At big recess we watched them eat
their greasy peas off tin
a tobacco-chewing white man over them
shotgun at the ready
and pistol slung
In class we'd hear them singing at their work
"Go Down Old Hannah"
"Jumpin Judy"
"Lead Me to the Rock"
I found a convict's filed off chain once in the woods
and took it home
and hid it

V

Tired of waiting for Hallowe'en
Jack and I had one ahead of time
and went round soaping windows
and chunking clods of mud on people's porches
Mr. Holcomb though came out shooting
his 45
at us scrouged up against a terrace
across the street
He meant to kill us too
because his fourth shot hit betwixt us
not a foot to spare each way
so we didn't wait for him to empty the magazine
but just aired out a mile a minute
Next day
our mothers made us apologize
and Mr. Holcomb said he wouldn't have shot at us
except it was so dark
he took us for nigger boys

VI

Confederate veterans came to town
for their convention
and tottered in parade

while Dixie played and everybody gave the rebel yell
but the Confederate burying ground near school
where the battle had been
nobody seemed to care about
It was a wilderness of weeds and brambles
with headstones broken and turned over
The big boys had a den in there
where they would drag the colored girls
that passed by on the path
and make them do
what they said all colored girls
liked doing
no matter how much
they fought back and screamed

VII

The Fourth of July
was a holiday for everybody but people's cooks
Corinne was fixing us hot biscuit
when I marched into the kitchen
waving the Stars and Stripes
and ordered her to
"Salute this flag! It made you free!"
I just couldn't understand why Corinne
plumb wouldn't

VIII

Old Major Suggs
ran for Public Safety Commissioner once
orating against the black menace
from his flag-draped touring car
and got just 67 votes
from a town that had 132,685 people in 1910
Things were well in hand back then
and folks were hard to panic
One night a chicken thief got into
old Major Suggs' hen-house
and made off with some of his Barred Rocks
The Major was slick
and figured out the path the thief was sure to take
back to niggertown
so he took a short cut through the woods
and hid behind a tree

The thief came staggering
beneath his sack of hens
and caught both barrels in his face
point-blank
"That nigger flopped and flopped"
old Major Suggs gloated long afterwards
"just like a big black rooster that you've axed"

    IX
Spurgeon would daub designs on flowerpots
wheelbarrows
garbage cans
just anything he could get his hands on
though all he had was house-paint
and the kind of big flat brush
you slap it on with
My mother said
Spurgeon was what you call
a primitive
One Saturday evening
he was downtown window-shopping the pawnshops
gawking at all the jewelry
the pretty knives and pistols
when a mob came tearing round the corner
after another black man
but they made Spurgeon do

YOU KIDDING OR SOMETHING WHITE FOLKS?

To the Messrs J. F. & Robt Kennedy Meany Udall et al
Sirs I have been stirred to the depths by your recent sonorous
pronouncements exhorting the populace to cease & desist from
discriminatory practices against Negroes & since I have no doubt
at all of your individual & collective sincerity I should like to call
to your notice an egregious instance of this evil against which you
so eloquently inveigh & which any one of you individually has

ample power to correct but collectively could instantly eradicate by a mere stroke of the pen as they say Well my wife & I were recently motoring through the "fair" state of Alabama when in our road rose gigantic the new Widow's Creek power plant of the TVA which is an agency of the U S Government Deciding to inspect this imposing facility my wife & I each took a most edifying leaflet from the guard (white) at the entry We proceeded to the visitors' gallery whence we commanded a view of the generators a long row of which were thrumming in unison except for one which was getting a new armature Electricians (white) swarmed antlike over the generator being repaired & as we were intently observing their activities a black employe of the U S of A came up to us pushing a broom over the spotless tiles of the gallery I smiled at him & he smiled back in friendly fashion & I asked him why he wasn't working down there on the generator with the electricians (white) & the broom-pushing black smilingly replied though with what I thought was a touch of irony "You kidding or something white folks?"

ON ACQUIRING A CISTERCIAN BREVIARY
For Father M. Louis, O.C.S.O.

Long cloistered these old volumes that my hands
profane. Rubbed spines spell golden seasons. *Pax
intrantibus!* How many hidden men
dipped honeycomb from hence and Samson-thewed
robustly strove till sepulture beside
the abbey church! Each has his sombre cross
of naked iron with laconic plaque,
sacerdos and *conversus* leveled quite,
Dom James whose tassel was abbatical
and bearded Frater Hyacinth who baked.
And will they rise triumphantly in choir
all faults expunged? These rubricated leaves
were thumbed by novices who now lie here.
But flowery tropes the prophecy and pledge,
a travesty on truth which holds no hope

for them? If so, how came they to be strong,
these silent monks? May desert rocks fill men
with food or venom work their cure? Embrace
such paradox who can. These books I'll have.

THE CAMALDOLESE COME TO BIG SUR

White-habited hermits pace fog that streams
landward at compline bell. The ambrosial coast
harbors flesh-eaters, a poet's evil dreams.
Their ordure smears the cliffs. Now Jeffers lies
earthfast save prayer of these ransom his ghost,
so avid of dark. Cowled fathers, exorcise
his doomed lovers. Asperse, blest hands, these great
headlands commanding sapphire plenitudes.
Where blood-stained phantoms neigh and ululate,
let seraphim deploy hushed multitudes.

FOUR HAIKU FOR PETER

1. *El Camposanto*
Rich graves crowd near the shrine,
dressed green. Poor lie far off
in Franciscan brown.

2. *Slum Gothic*
Great empty nave.
Worship rocks store-fronts.
Peter's barque stranded on a reef.

3. *After Holy Communion*
Ite, missa est. Wealth
of cleanliness pours out.
Streets awash with filth.

4. *Picketing Hell Gate*
"Thou Shalt Not Kill!" Stand,
girl at the missile plant. Let men mock.
Stay His hand.

SELF PORTRAIT IN A BAD LIGHT

My stripling authors flee the room to rub
congenial elbows in those dives where false
identities will pass. Cassocks withdraw
to contemplation of reforms. (But not
too radical nor yet too near the quick
of clerical privilege!) Dare I adjure
my Muse to plain of social wrongs in such
precarious circumstance? Must I be schooled,
veil plain speech in symbolic fog, costume
polemics for a merry morris dance,
practice new types of ambiguity,
and baffle those who sniff out heresy?
These shifts are common to the trade and steer
the prudent to snug haven when the gale's
a-starboard, blustery. No matter. The old
dog's teeth, to vary tropes, grow blunt. His eye
is blear. He shows more energy in dreams,
waggling his paws, then questing on all fours.
Who would heed his bark, grown querulous and faint?

PUNTA DE LOS LOBOS MARINOS

He'd crawled up in the cove to die alone.
When we came near he raised his head, his eyes
blank disks. Flies fed on pus that dripped from them.
Flies swarmed upon his flippers. Feverish,
he shook. "There's nothing we can do but let
old nature take her course," the ranger said
and sauntered off. The young sea lion dropped
his heavy head and coughed sepulchrally.
"Pneumonia," I ventured. "He needs a shot."
"I'd give him one," a man remarked, "except
he'd sink his teeth in me." "You're an M.D.?"
"That's right," he said. "I'll hold him for you then."
I gripped that bullet head with both my hands.
Hide bent the needle double but the dose
went in, good for a week. The creature roared
as youngsters do when stuck. The doctor wiped
his ruined needle. "Can't do harm," he said,
"and maybe he'll get well." Next day the beach
was bare. The pack was sunning on the rocks
offshore. Some slithered in the Caldron's rips,
outwitting clashing seas and granite teeth.
We guessed one lucky youngster was home free.

ONE MORE RIVER TO CROSS
For John L. Salter, Jr.

"The passage of the Patowmac through the Blue Ridge"
wrote the author of the Declaration of Independence
"is one of the most stupendous scenes in nature"
In the midst of this stupendous scene
on the second day of December 1859
the sovereign state of Virginia

hanged old Osawatomie Brown
(strange confluence of rivers)
for holding certain truths to be self-evident
which had been first enunciated
by the greatest Virginian of them all
A bystander at the hanging
one Thomas J Jackson
was struck by the incongruity of Brown's
"white socks and slippers of predominating red"
beneath sober black garb more appropriate to the occasion
A frivolous touch that "predominating red"
or could it have been a portent
Thomas J soon-to-be-dubbed "Stonewall" Jackson?
"Across the river and into the trees" you babbled
only four years later
while your blood ebbed away
ironically shot by one of your own
But it is still the second of December 1859
and you glowing with the vigor of a man in his prime
are watching while the body of Brown swings slowly
to and fro
in a cold wind off the mountains
for exactly 37 minutes before it is cut down
In less than half so many months
Thomas J Jackson
this stupendous scene plus 24,000 contiguous square miles
will no longer be Virginia
Its blue-uniformed sons will be ranged against you
in the Army of the Potomac singing
"John Brown's body lies a-mouldering in the grave
but his soul goes marching on"

Now you my friend
so akin in spirit to the earlier John
I have been seeing your picture in the papers
your head anointed with mustard and ketchup
at the lunch-counter sit-in
hoodlums rubbing salt in the cuts where they slugged you
or the police flailing you with clubs
blood sopping your shirt
but pure downright peace on your face
making a new kind of history
Now the people Harper's Weekly called

"this good-humored good-for-nothing half monkey race"
when John Brown sought to lead them out of bondage
are leading us toward that America
Thomas Jefferson foresaw and Abraham Lincoln
who once again sprawls dying in his theatre box
(Why must we always kill our best?)
The dastard in the bushes spots the crossed hairs
squeezes the trigger and Medgar Evers pitches
forward on his face while the assassin scuttles
into the night his beady rat's eyes seeking where to hide
his incriminating weapon with the telescopic sight
He heaves it into the tangled honeysuckle
and vanishes into the magnolia darkness
"God Sees the Truth But Waits"
The sickness is loosed now into the whole body politic
the infection spreading from South to North and West
"States Rights" "Freedom of Choice" "Liberty of the Individual"
Trojan horse phrases with armed enemies within
In the name of rights they would destroy all rights
put freedom to death on the pretext of saving it
Under the cover of Jeffersonian verbiage
these men move to destroy the Constitution
they feign to uphold
but their plots will miscarry
Who knows but that some unpainted shack in the Delta
may house one destined to lead us the next great step of the way
From the Osawatomie to the "Patowmac"
the Alabama Tombigbee Big Black Tallahatchie and Pearl
and down to the Mississippi levee in Plaquemines Parish
it's a long road
better than a hundred years in traveling
and now the Potomac again . . .

Summer, 1963

ESCORT FOR A PRESIDENT

I

Rapt to our screens we watch him borne inert
and casketed into the plane he stepped
from a few hours ago invulnerable,
serene and radiant. Young Zeus he seemed
at breakfast, brandishing his thunderbolts
and vaunting of the billions he'd dispensed
to Texans slavering for contracts. Votes
he angled for with grisly bait but was
first casualty of his dread TFX
although the instrument which took his life
was obsolete as bow and arrow. Lord,
Thine irony is more cruel than Thy wrath.

II

The land's sad face averts itself, now bleak
and sere that's starred with blue bonnets in spring
and Dallas underwing diminishes,
the azure shafts that oil and cattle built,
the marts where Santa holds his blazing court.
Small Jesús flattens nose upon plate glass
but José's out of work and so is María.

III

Assumed into a myth more speedily
than Lincoln was or Roosevelt he floats
across the fabled river so far down
it seems the life-line on some ancient palm.
Mortality is sloughed in upper air
above the Mississippi. Brooding here
another myth circles on eagle wings
biding its time. Crossed hairs upon a back
as on a head brought to a baleful term
two young men's lives. Medgar, here's company.

IV

Now swarming up the air with cries like doves
or angels come black girls from Birmingham
with blood upon their Sunday finery
and faces blown away. Here also wheel

two black boys slain in cleanlier wise by bullets
upon that Sabbath day. May they escort
a president upon his journey home?

A COMMEMORATIVE ODE

For the 60th Anniversary of the Beecher Memorial United Church of Christ in New Orleans, Louisiana, October 25, 1964

Old church with the same name as my own
you and I were born in the same year
It has taken two generations to bring us together
Now here we are in New Orleans
meeting for the first time
I hope I can say the right thing
what the man you are named for
might have said on one of his better days
He was my great-great-uncle
but come to think of it
he was instrumental in my founding too
Rolled in a tube at home I have a certificate
signed by Henry Ward Beecher
after he had united my grandfather and grandmother
in the holy bonds of matrimony
at Plymouth Church in Brooklyn
The year was 1858
and James Buchanan was President
The South was riding high
making the North catch and send back its escaped Negroes
and it looked to most people
as if slavery were going to last forever
but not to Henry Ward Beecher
which I suppose is why you named your church for him
He certainly helped to change all that
together with his brother Edward and his sister

whose name was Harriet
and Mr. Lincoln and General Ulysses S. Grant
and a large number of young men
who wound up under the long rows of crosses
at Gettysburg Chickamauga Cold Harbor and such places

Nineteen hundred and four was a better year
than 1858
and the building of this church was a sign of it
It was no longer a crime to meet and worship by yourselves
with your own preacher
your own beautiful songs
with no grim-lipped regulators to stand guard over you
nobody breaking up your services with a bull-whip
Yes this was some better
Booker T. Washington was in his hey-day
the apostle of segregation
"We can be in all things social as separate as the fingers"
he said and Mr. Henry Grady the Atlanta editor
applauded him to the echo
as did all the other good white folks around
and they said
"This boy Booker has a head on his shoulders
even if it is a nappy one"
Dr. Washington was 48 years old at the time
but you know how southern whites talk
a man is a boy all his life if he's black
Dr. Washington was a pragmatist
and settled for what he could get
When they announced that dinner was served in the dining car
he ate his cindery biscuits out of a paper bag
and when George the porter made up berths in the Pullman
he sat up all night in the Jim Crow coach
Because of his eminently practical attitude
Dr. Washington was successful in shaking down
the big white philanthropists
like C. P. Huntington the railroad shark
or was it octopus
and Negro education was on its way

Old church
since 1904
you and I have seen some changes

slow at first
now picking up speed
I have just come from Mississippi
where I saw churches like this one
burned to the ground
or smashed flat with bombs
almost like Germany when I was there in 1945
only these Negroes were not beaten people
They sang in the ashes and wreckage
such songs as *We Shall Overcome*
and *Let My Little Light Shine*
O Freedom! they sang
Before I'll be a slave
I'll be buried in my grave
and go home to my Lord and be free
They sang *I'm going to sit at the welcome table*
I'm going to live in the Governor's mansion
one of these days
I heard three mothers speak
who had made the President listen
and "almost cry, or he made like he was about to cry"
when they told him
how their homes had been dynamited
"It's not hard to be brave"
one of these mothers said
"but it's awful hard to be scared"
I expect to see her statue on a column in the square
in place of the Confederate soldier's
one of these days .

Remember
slavery looked pretty permanent in 1858
when it had just five years to go
and now in 1964
the White Citizens' Councils and the Ku Klux Klan
think they can keep their kind of half-slave South forever
Their South isn't on the way out
It's already dead and gone
only they don't know it
They buried it themselves
in that earthwork dam near Philadelphia Mississippi
when they thought they were getting rid of the bodies

WOKE UP THIS MORNING WITH MY MIND SET ON FREEDOM

A flood of song
breaches the levee
swamps cabins in the cotton
sweeps Natchez-under-the-hill

The flock escapes old shepherds
who in the dust of the stampede
incredulous and dazed
lumber along out of breath

Frock coats and crinolines
built nothing here
but skilled black hands
reared all this beauty

Which one of these
white-colonnaded bastions of the ancient lie
among moss-oaks and magnolias
will be our Freedom House?

Natchez during the demonstrations, September, 1965

SOMEBODY WINS

Rain pelts the plastic-sheeted heap beside
the highway. One blue tennis shoe protrudes,
child-size. No child's the curving hip of her
mangled beneath, her car a jagged wreck.
The flinders of a second strew the swamp,
where moss-hung cypresses droop dankly down.
Attendants lead its blinded driver toward
the ambulance. Blood oozes from his lids.
Two cameras always at the ready, my
free-lancing friend leaps out and films the heap,

blue tennis shoe, the oozing lids, the feet
of spectators slogging around the corpse.
He climbs back in and we roar off again.
"That was a lucky break!" my friend exults.

THE CONVICT MINES
Circa 1910

"You sho' God bettah dig yo' task lessen
dat sweat-box git you or yo' bones be foun'
down some ole shaft." At dawn the shackled men,
lamps flaring on their caps, rode underground.
Four bits a day each convict brought on lease,
leading astute police to engineer
crap games to raid. Feeding just pone and peas,
mine owners heaped up fortunes year by year.
Murderers proved most reliable trusties
to stimulate output, wielding the thong
on shirkers and the sick alike. The fees
kept taxes down. Few deemed the system wrong,
it worked so well. Crime profited the state
and reinforced the black mortality rate.

MAN OF HONOR

His black barouche swept down the avenue
from his Ionic mansion's porte-cochere,
brisk hooves sounding matutinal tattoo.
Honeysuckle upon sequestered air
giving place to the aroma of pit privies,
he rode, scented silk handkerchief to nose,
by his abutting Negro properties

which squatted rump to rump in squalid rows.
Alighting at his bank's grave porticoes,
our subject laid aside *noblesse oblige*
during banking hours, though never would he foreclose
upon a social equal. Who'd then presage,
himself foreclosed in '29, his shame
would dictate that he sign in blood quit-claim?

DIXIE BARD

The inexorable anapests of Dixie bard
Stella Foxhall DeRoulhac rode to rescue
white womanhood from brutish blacks. She charred
foiled rapists in slow fires as surely due.
Maternal cares oft frustrating her Muse,
Stella conveyed her daughter's custody
to a half-witted maid. The wench was loose
but never asked for Sundays off at three.
People, said Stella, were just pampering maids.
The half-wit in the bushes held Love's court
when school let out and soon the primary grades
practiced precociously the eldest sport.
Young Stella, barely six, showed future promise
of nymphomania, nor did prediction miss.

SILENT IN DARIEN

He glimpses through dividing wire gold thighs
and shameless buttocks of *señoras gringas*
at play like children on the grass, his hell
their paradise. Bloat-bellied, puny sex
exposed, his brood clamors about the shack

tin-cans and cartons built. Girls who survive
turn assets, spreading rachitic legs to ease
off-duty Yanqui personnel. His sons
besides the pimping trade will follow such
pursuits as untaught hands may ply for rice
and beans, fare foreordained, lucky those days
they feed. In crystal shrines across the fence
one sees prime cuts of beef—*por Dios!*—milk,
the precious nuggets of the hen enclosed
in cunning boxes, bins of liquors, sweets,
rare nutriments whose flavors, even names
are mysteries, done up in shimmering foil.
The sky goes black as when a hurricane
lowers from the Caribbean. Unobscured
the sun glows bloody red. There will be wind.

IF I FORGET THEE, O BIRMINGHAM!

I
Like Florence from your mountain.
Both cast your poets out
for speaking plain.

II
You bowl your bombs down aisles
where black folk kneel
to pray for your blacker souls.

III
Dog-torn children bled
A, B, O, AB as you.
Christ's blood not more red.

IV
Burning my house to keep
them out, you sowed wind. Hear it blow!
Soon you reap.

KID PUNCH

Uptown by the Longshoremen's Hall
the Kid has a kind of kennel out back of a house
where he sleeps and does his little cooking
of the few things the doctor still lets him have
and waits for the phone to ring
He was one of the very first to take the music upriver
and played with Jelly Roll in Chicago
admits he was the "drinkines' man in the world"
but nobody blew a greater trumpet
You can still tell from the phrasing of his solos
but the power's not there any more
The Kid's over seventy with a bad heart hypertension
diabetes ulcers you name it he has got it
The other old musicians claw him down
"His lip is gone"
and shake gray heads over his senility
"Me, I'll quit when I gits like him"
When the Kid's phone does ring
it's usually late in the day
like he was a fill-in for the man they really wanted
no time to get his lip in shape
so when he blows it swells to twice its size
The Kid rings me up sometimes
"You come across any people on your trips
needs a band to play for 'em
don't forget me
Charge 'em ninety or a hundred dollars
and give eighty to the band
You could make yourself some money"

SOME OLD CREOLE CUSTOMS

My white New Orleans friends
had a black friend
who couldn't come into one of the white bars
for a drink with them
so they went into a black bar with him
taking a chance on the cops
Almost at once two of them came in
and grabbing my white friends' black friend
dragged him out on the sidewalk
where they started whipping him about the head
with their pistol butts
which in case you don't know is
an old Creole custom like Mardi Gras
Now Oscar one of my white friends became
quite incensed over the treatment of his black friend
by the jack-booted pride of New Orleans
and non-violently put in his two-bits worth
whereupon a pistol butt crashed his skull
and when he came to he was being hustled
by the seat of his pants to a squad car
where his black friend already lay
unconscious on the floor
"Where are you taking my husband?"
rhetorically queried Oscar's wife Chloe
and the gallant boys in blue replied
"To prison madame where we have accommodations
for you as well if you will be so good
as to accompany us" and wrastled her into the car
Chloe was extended
some of that fine old hospitality
for which the Crescent City is famed
They placed her in a cell apart from her husband
in the section reserved for Negro males
who it turned out
were all gentlemen
while all the rest of the night the white police
strutted up and down in front of her cell
hefting their manly parts
"Lady like some of this?
It's better than nigger stuff"

BLACK AND WHITE TOGETHER

"We were with you at heart
but you see
we couldn't do anything about it
we would have been expelled from college
That's why
we weren't out there on the streets with you
It really made us feel terrible
when we saw it on TV
the fire-hoses
the police dogs
the clubbings and all that
but there wasn't a thing we could do"
"You mean now it's different
Now you are ready to join us?
You know it's your freedom too
We aren't just fighting for our own
We're going to picket next week"

"Well the Dean says
the college has still got that regulation
He says it's for our protection as well as theirs
so I guess we can't make it
but our hearts are with you
Really
we want you to know that"

Birmingham, 1965

GEORGIA SCENE: 1964

And so this cat
he was from the GBI
that's the cracker FBI
kept feeling up the chicks' legs with his electric cattle prod
and making them wiggle and holler

He couldn't get enough of that stuff
poking that hot thing up under they dresses
and I be dog
if one of them cracker polices
didn't break down and cry like a baby
just watching him
but he didn't try to stop him
no I guess that would be too much to expect of any cracker
I disremember all the meanness that they did
treating them Yankees like they was us
dragging that 70-year-old white lady
down the courthouse steps
with her head going bam on every step
Her heart give out
and the ambulance came
but when the driver saw she was
one of them agitators
he just took off again and left her laying in the street
Finally one of us took her to the hospital
propped up in the back seat of a car
but wouldn't no white doctor touch her when she got there
Had to find one of ours
and put her in the Jim Crow section
Sure ain't like no ofays I ever knowed
coming down here and getting they heads beat for nothing
trying to love these crackers into being Christian
like crackers was human

DE AMICITIA *UPDATED*

Prize your old friends, saith Holy Writ. The text's
Ecclesiasticus, IX, 10. New friends
are likened unto wine that's new, best kept
encasked for ripening. How obsolete
the maxims of the Scriptures grow! When used,
discard your friends. Such figures as yourselves,

wardens of white hegemony, do well
to shun those intimates whose unsound views
diverge from yours on the Great Question. *Vale,*
my quondam friends who found my father's whiskey
a potent spur to amity, who at
our charge sojourned in balsam boughs or by
the breakers' edge, vowing your fealty
while privately confiding in us deep
solicitude for one another. "Poor
Lucius! I fear his reason is unhinged.
Only an angel could put up with him!"
"Mark's so well-mannered that you'd never guess
his mother kept a common boarding-house.
I doubt Eugenia would have married him
if she had known. Perhaps that's why she topes."
But you, my trusty *Doppelgänger,* you
who capped my ribaldries with better. Often
we queued for Orphic pleasures in the snow,
then thawed among the girders of our four-
bit heaven. Strings, horns, woodwinds, tympani
straggled upon the stage. Seraphic Serge
ascended to the podium and poised
his marvelous baton. Blot all the rest.
But the Firebird! The Posthorn Serenade!

AS GOOD AS GOLD

My father had an office all to himself with SECRETARY &
     TREASURER lettered on the glass door a big mahogany desk
          and twin brass spittoons which I never saw him use
First thing every morning Abraham Lincoln Summerall would
     shuffle deferentially into my father's office wearing a
          white coat and carrying a shoe-shine kit
Kneeling as to a white idol black Abe would add new luster
     to my father's already lustrous shoes
Abe never shined the shoes of my father's chief assistants
     nor of the numerous other white men in my father's department

since this would have constituted *lese majeste*
As the office porter and the only black man on the entire
   fourteenth floor Abe had to watch his P's and Q's
If there was a package to be toted Abe toted it and no white
   employe of the TCI & RR Co was ever seen to be encumbered
   by a burden of any description
Abe often accompanied the Paymaster Mr Manfred Gordon
   to the Birmingham Trust returning with twin satchels
     of currency and coin while hard-eyed white guards
     convoyed him with Winchesters and 38 Specials
It couldn't have been that they didn't trust Abe with the coin
   and the currency because everybody in the Treasury department
   including my father said Abe was "as good as gold"
Which among that particular class of white men was the highest
   compliment a black man could be paid
Mr Manfred Gordon the Paymaster was on the other hand
   what is commonly known as a "perfect Southern gentleman"
He loved his dear old mother from Virginia to such an inordinate
   extent that he courted Miss Lucy Haynes the florist for
     better than 20 years but never married her lest he
     hurt his mother's feelings
Unquestionably Mr Manfred Gordon was a man of the most tender
   sensibilities where women were concerned but with men
     black men that is
He was different
Mr Manfred Gordon would take my grandfather who was a retired
   Episcopal rector and me a small boy on all-day paycar trips
     out to the steel mills ore mines and coal mines
My grandfather laughed till the silver pectoral cross he wore
   over his black silk vest jumped like crazy
To hear Mr Manfred Gordon cussing the black men he paid off
   for no-count black bastards and sons of bitches as they
     filed by the window to get their envelopes of money
My grandfather though the descendant of noted Abolitionists
   was a broadminded clergyman who had adjusted to the
     Southern way of life and he would even take a toddy
     with Mr Manfred Gordon when the day was done
I thought it somewhat strange in my boyish naïveté that
   Mr Manfred Gordon cussed only the black and never the
     white men who filed by his pay window and I supposed
     it was because he was such a perfect Southern gentleman
Many years later after the big stock market crash in 1929
   Mr Manfred Gordon jumped out of a window on the 14th floor
   thoughtfully choosing one on the court side

Being such a perfect Southern gentleman he wished to avoid
    the great scandal which would have been occasioned
        had he jumped into the street
Mr Manfred Gordon's body landed on a rooftop instead of
    the pavement and my father sent Abe Summerall to retrieve it
        since it was Abe's duty as office porter to carry bundles

REPORT TO HEROD

Sir, resistance was encountered
from a bomb crater made by a B-52
and so a private in my patrol
threw a grenade into the crater
but somebody threw it back and it blew up
and injured three of my men
I went myself then and took a grenade
pulled the pin and held it just long enough
before lobbing it into the crater
That put an end to the resistance
we checked in there
and found one dead VC baby
three VC kids also dead
and two VC women one still living with her left leg blown off
Sir, the chaplain asked me
if I'd serve Mass for him again tomorrow
OK, sir, if I go?

VIATICUM

It was a heartfelt confession
perhaps the most contrite I ever heard
I found a small spot on his cheek
where I could anoint him
all the rest of his poor body being burned

His death I think was happy
but what a pity
just twenty-two
his life ahead of him
A human torch
He said we'd burned so many with our napalm
he wanted us to know
what it was really like
Fantastic how the young
get things mixed up
It comes from reading
but he repented honestly
and made a Christian end

PRAY FOR WAR

My troop roped back the cheering crowd at First
and Twentieth where four skyscrapers stood,
"the heaviest corner in the South" postcards
of Birmingham proclaimed. Our own Rainbow
Division, bound for France, swung by behind
its banners and its bands. My boyish heart
was sore, though not for men about to die,
myself sole object of my own compassion.
Head scout of all the troop, my chest ablaze
with merit badges and insignia,
more stripes upon my sleeve than any boy's,
I cursed the fate that made me but thirteen.
Why had my parents been so derelict,
wedded five years before engendering
their only son? Each night I prayed that God
would keep the carnage going until I
could join the "Devil Dogs" at seventeen,
just four more years. (My dad promised consent.)
My prayers were answered though belatedly
and my appointment with the god of war
came round in time. Prayer never fails. Nor will

it fail you, boys, who yearn to emulate
the deeds of bombardiers and Green Berets,
your hearts aflame as mine was once to share
the rites of holocaust. You'll get your turn.

A HOUSE DIVIDED

Half Cherokee, half black, Emma despised
her African ancestors whom she thought
half animal. She bleached her skin and prized
her long straight hair. No black man ever caught
Emma in mood for love. Caucasian seed
alone won entrance to her womb. The fruit
was blue-eyed Cora, honey-hued, indeed
a goddess though her ways were dissolute
and she was jailed for knifing a white lover.
Emma worshipped her daughter all the same.
Her mistress often scolded Emma over
her clamorous broils with the kitchen crew. Hot shame
filled Emma. "I cain't he'p it!" So always ran
her plea. "It's mah daddy in me, ole nigguh man!"

SUTTEE

She was the perfect servant, they believed,
with no thought for herself but only them
and their higher concerns. Georgie relieved
old Mrs Jukes of everything, a gem.
Miss Mae was not allowed to make her bed
nor vacuum her room nor wash a dish.
Languid and bored, Mae brought the man she wed

as great a bargain as a fool might wish.
Georgie at last was given her *congé*.
Broken by overwork and age, she cared
for Sim, her syphilitic man, who lay
speechless and blind, yet beat her when he dared.
First axing Sim, she set their shack afire
and slit her throat upon her widow's pyre.

THE CHAUTAUQUA

I

Great Commoner

Their iron-tired wagon wheels grating
on the raw bricks awakened her at daybreak.
All morning they rolled in from the tall corn,
the prairie folk, red-faced and sober-sided,
for this was Bryan's day in Egypt. Around
the big top wagons filled the field but still
their streams debouched down every black mud track
from Karnak, Olive Branch, Lickcreek and Buncombe.
The July sun climbed up the implacable sky
of Illinois, turning the circus tent
into a huge and sweltering oven where
the sweating multitudes on folding chairs
waved palm-leaf fans, awaiting the silver tongue
to peal its mystic message to their ears:
"You shall not press on labor's brow this crown
of thorns; you shall not crucify mankind
upon a cross of gold!" The managers
in panic sought my mother, though her turn
to declaim a Shakespearean play entire
was not scheduled until that night. "For God's
sake help us out! Please come and entertain them!
The tent's already full and he's not due
till noon!" The five thousand upturned faces
stirred her to tears, transfigured as they were

by expectation of the Messiah. What might
she substitute to slake their need of him?
"Tomorrow and tomorrow and tomorrow
Creeps in this petty pace from day to day
To the last syllable of recorded time
And all our yesterdays have lighted fools
The way to dusty death"? That wouldn't do!
"The barge she sat in, like a burnished throne,
Glowed on the water"? Wrong Egypt. Jaques
the melancholy? "All the world's a stage
And all the men and women merely players;
They have their exits and their entrances;
And one man in his time plays many parts"?
Hardly the proper text to preface Bryan
the incorruptible, sworn enemy
of Wall Street and the wicked Eastern trusts.
She chose what seemed most fit, the Hoosier bard's
"Little Orphant Annie" and "The Raggedy Man,"
conjuring cooling visions with "When the Frost
is on the Punkin," making them weep with Field
for Little Boy Blue's untimely end and all
his battered toys still to be put away.
Then a murmur rose like wind in the ripe corn
and grew to a roar as the rotund prophet
stalked up to the platform. "Bryan, it's Bryan!"

II

Fighting Bob

The Honorable Robert M. LaFollette
each summer followed the Chautauqua circuit.
The Senator had a crowd-pleasing act
that rivaled the feats of the Swiss bell-ringers
according to my mother who traveled
in the same troupe with that great statesman
and other luminaries of less note.
This act came in the midst of his set speech
excoriating railroads, banks, steel trust,
meat packers, Standard Oil and other foes
of the people. Mounting to a crescendo
"Fighting Bob" would choke with righteous fury
detailing the dastardly deeds of these reptiles
and finding the stricture binding his throat too much
to tolerate further would at the exact same phrase

in his speech every night seize in both hands
his celluloid collar and rip it from his neck
while his ready-tied bow sailed across the platform
trailing its rubber band. My mother said
she wouldn't have minded it so much if just
the Senator had varied the timing once.

III

1912 Overture

My mother was the queen of all the troupe
and I the mascot. The Quartet that sang
"Little Brown Church in the Wildwood" adopted me
and so did J. Adam Bede, the Congressman
from Minnesota's Iron Range, whose deep
and booming voice offset his dwarfishness
and gave the lie to sneering Emil Seidel,
the Socialist Mayor of Milwaukee, who
in their nightly debates declared that Bede
was J. P. Morgan's henchman on the Range.
I should have paid more heed to Seidel but
I lacked a sense of history at eight
and took men at face value. Bede was jolly.
He told me jokes while Seidel never spoke
at table. Crush the adders young he must
have thought. My father worked for the Steel Trust.
Seidel maintained that Socialism would
rule all the earth some day while J. Adam Bede
claimed private enterprise had been ordained
by the Almighty. I listened till I fell
asleep bolt upright in my folding chair.
I wasn't the only one. When Mother read
a play nobody fell asleep. You could
hear that proverbial pin drop any time
or watches ticking in men's pockets. She
was beautiful and shining on the platform
and I was proud to be her little boy.
"A poor thing but mine own," she'd say of me
and I'd agree. It was our private joke.
We crossed High Bridge, Kentucky, on the train
and rode a stern-wheel steamboat up the Coosa
River. One happy family I guess
we were on the Chautauqua that summer
of 1912 except for Mayor Seidel.

A LITERARY MEMOIR: 1939

Tom Collins was my new friend's name
though not his drink. My silver dollar spun
across the bar. "Two double Scotches."
He drank and then went on. "The bastard put
me in the book. The little manager.
That's me at Weed Patch Camp. By Jesus Christ
we jumped through hoops for him. I put him in
a tent just like he was another Okie.
Sent all the folks with stories in to talk.
They trusted me. I told 'em, 'Look,
this guy may be a writer but he's on our side.
Spill everything.' Dozens of notebooks full
he got before he left to write the book.
Fine book too. I ain't denying that.
Dedicated it to me and Carol.
*To CAROL who willed this book. To TOM
who lived it.* If you want to, check it out.
That TOM is me, me by God. Took me to Hollywood.
Says to me, 'I want you for the technical adviser,
see they don't phony up the film but keep
it true to life.' Two hundred bucks a week
I got while they were shooting. Christ knows
how much he got out of the film and all
those millions of copies of the book. So what
does he do then? He buys himself a ranch
up in the Coast Range mountains. Fancy place.
Swimming pool. Builds him a great big fence
and hangs up a sign to beware of the dog.
How you like that for a 'people's novelist'?
You know that crap they write about him, don't you?
Revolutionary, my big toe. Just wait.
You'll see. Right off the bat he ditched us all.
I mean the folks who spilled their guts to him.
Won't even let us in the gate no more.
Next thing you know he'll ditch Carol too.
I saw him down in Hollywood. Those bitches!"
Another dollar spun across the bar.

OLD PRESBYTER WRIT SMALL
For F. W. B. 1835–1919

A silver Celtic cross adorned his black
silk dickey while a Roman collar spanned
his neck. In no wise did he seem to lack
canonical faculties and yet they banned
him from baptizing me. A heretic,
my own grandfather! The One True Church had ways
inscrutable. Alas, poor Frederick,
you'd still be banned these ecumenical days.
Robert Perdue and I would drive him round
Sundays to the Episcopalian church to preach,
then sit outside. Never did dogma unsound
or tinged with Anglican error make a breach
in my defenses. Hearing such was sin
while Rob was black. Neither might go in.

A DOG'S LIFE AND SOME OTHERS

Jack was the smartest dog in town, or so I thought,
and I had evidence. My Dad and I took him
along for company on our Sunday hikes. We'd end
twelve long miles from home in Bessemer or East Lake
and ride the street car back, leaving poor wistful Jack
to get home by his nose. He'd always beat us there,
having outrun the trolley, and greet us joyfully
as if he feared we were the ones who had got lost.

Once though Jack dragged himself home with a bullet clean
through both hind legs and penis. In a week or so
he was as good as new. No one ever saw him run
from any other dog until the Ransoms' hound
that Jack despised and would run out of his own yard
took after Jack one day with muzzle dripping foam
and chased him all the way home but when Jack arrived
on his own territory he turned and stood his ground.

They say smart dogs will always run from a mad one
but Jack drew the line at running from his own yard.
It was the most terrific dog fight I ever saw
and people gathered, yelling, "Mad dog! Somebody kill him!"
I dashed in the house and got my Dad's big pistol
meaning to shoot the mad dog before he killed Jack
but a man wrestled me down and snatched the gun off me
because I was kind of small for the job at six

They broke the fight up with a bucket of water.
Somebody else got to shoot the mad dog. They shipped
his head off to the State Veterinarian
while I had to keep Jack locked up in the cellar
till the lab report came back from Montgomery.
It was rabies all right. What else would Jack have run from?
He hadn't gone mad yet. Just to be safe they put
Jack to sleep and made me take the Pasteur treatment.

Dr Morton stuck a needle in my stomach
twenty-one straight days. Because I didn't flinch or cry
he said I was the bravest boy he'd ever seen
not knowing how most nights I cried into my pillow
over Jack. He was so gentle with that needle
I grew fond of Dr Morton. I grew even fonder
later of his daughter but she preferred whiskey
so in the end the doctor put himself to sleep.

OUR LADY OF THE SNOW
For I.G.B., September 26, 1867–
December 30, 1955

Snapping the frail synapses one by one
the tendrils from her heart hardened and burst
till all her spirit's harmonies were still.
We watched the slow extinguishing of what
had warmed us like the great diurnal sun.

Unready souls, we shivered in the chill.
The drudge who mopped excretions, changed and nursed
her fled the agony and died insane.
My father in his tent gulped oxygen.
Summoned, I sat and held my mother's hand
and heard the sounds as fluids filled her lungs.
A poem that she'd written long ago
came back to me. "I cannot go," she had
foretold, "if it is raining." All that night
the rain roared down to mock her. Thus she died.
Into a dank and alien darkness I
went stumbling to my bed. The risen sun
awoke me to a glittering world. Fresh snow,
white for her feast, vested the Santa Cruz range.

IN COMMUNICATION WITH THE ENEMY

Elias Fries, my father's closest friend,
of Swedish origin though naturalized,
and Annerika, his likewise Swedish wife,
had small regard for Birmingham's opinion.
In the First War they endowed an ambulance
but stipulated that the Swiss Red Cross
should operate it for the benefit
of all belligerents who fell upon
the blood-soaked fields of Belgium and of France,
suspicious neutralism in the view
of Christian Birmingham. An engineer
was Fries, one of the very best around,
who built steel mills to roll out armor plate
and shells. A useful man but dangerous.
The Vigilance Committee kept an eye
upon his mail. Postmarked from Sweden came
one day a German publication no one
could read, except the title, *Theory
of Relativity*. The author was a Hun

named Albert Einstein and the work contained
a mass of formulae and other junk
that threw the profs from Tuscaloosa. Code,
they all pronounced it. Fries was haled
before the Vigilance Committee. "You're in
communication with the enemy!"
They spurned his fishy tale of how it was
a purely scientific work he'd asked
his brother in Sweden to procure for him
because of its significance. They would
have packed Fries off to prison on the spot
except the corporation couldn't spare him.
Suppose that Fries's rolling mills broke down?
What would they do for armor plate and shells?

A LUCKY NIGHT IN 1920

That splotch on the rubbled brick is blood. New on
the job, the boy sat down and fell asleep.
No clearance there. The charging car shredded
his bones. The Bessemers are blowing billows
of crashing flame. I race through glittering spray
with orders for the melter. "Titanic" slaps
my smouldering sweater out. "Think you're a God
damn Roman candle, kid?" Dark blue glasses
are perched on his forehead. Shoving them down,
"Titanic" squats at Number Four's peepholes.
The slag creams pink above the seething steel.
Old Man John the melter gropes for his dime-
store specs, then reads his orders at arm's length.
"Heat's sahft as shit," he says. "Won't mek rail-steel.
Tell that night super he cahn kiss me ahss,"
and puffing on his stogie he rolls off
as if on wheels. A north wind sweeps the mill.
I back against the furnace to get warm
and go to sleep upon my feet. Hubbub

jars me awake, yells and a floor-crane's jangling
alarm. Waving his arms is Old Man John.
"Dahm boy, run for your blahsted life!" Blinding
white steel is pouring from a burn-through just
behind me. In one great leap I cross the floor
and duck behind the tin tool-shack just as
the main water line explodes. Live steam, shot through
with molten streaks, fills all the mill with light.
Salvoes of glowing bricks batter my shield.

REQUIESCAT

Requiescat . . . they touch the burnished wood
in tribute to their fallen prince as if . . .
as if . . . as if he might (had he but lived)
have brought back the Golden Age new garnished
with the palms of a lasting peace. Look! Black
and white together like in the song we used to sing
until too many false notes soured it in our ears.
Would he perhaps have made it sound once more
invincible and true? As if we meant
it? Meant to build belated justice here?
And could see it with wide open eyes? Troops
once more descending gangplanks on home shores,
an end to hecatombs upon our screens,
the heaped-up dead, weeping mothers, bandaged
babies, wrecked towns, remorseless tanks and planes?
Might we have seen ghettoes blown up instead,
new homes for human beings rising there,
great parks and schools, wealth used not to destroy
but build a decent world? This was his dream.
He might have faltered in the savage fight
which lay ahead. He might have been undone
by his inherent weaknesses. Too rich,
some felt he was, too privileged. We must
forgive him for the things he couldn't help.
We touch the burnished wood and turn again
to face the daylight, pitilessly clear.

A HUMBLE PETITION
TO THE PRESIDENT OF HARVARD

I am, sir, so to speak, "a Harvard man."
In legendary times I lugged my green
baize bag across the Yard to sit while fierce
Professor Kittredge paced his podium
in forkéd snowy beard and pearl-gray spats,
mingling his explications with his views
obscurantist on life and letters. Texts
prescribed for us were caponized. Prince Hamlet
made no unseemly quips anent the thighs
Ophelia spread for him nor did that poor
crazed beauty sing the naughty songs for which
she's celebrated. Nice young men were we
in Kitty's class. Extra-curricular
our smut—Old Howard queens of bump and grind,
the Wellesley girls who warmed our chambers. Such
the Harvard I recall: Widener's great hive,
whose honeyed lore we rifled and bore off
on index cards, all nutriment destroyed;
the home of Henry Wadsworth Longfellow;
dank mournful halls; an ill-proportioned pile
commemorating boys who'd marched away
to die for causes the professors had
endorsed, knowing infallibly which side
God and their butter were upon. Our boot-
legger was Polish. Christened Casimir
Zwijacz he'd changed his name to Lawrence Lowell
after fair Harvard's president. Ambushed
and shot by high-jackers who coveted
his rot-gut load, Lowell barrelled his truck
back from Cape Cod and, bandaged bloodily,
made punctual deliveries to all
his Cambridge clientele, fresh lustre shed
upon an honored name. *Per aspera!*
Nostalgic reminiscences brought on
by your most recent bulletin. I learn
of your "Commitment to the Modern," penned
expressly for Old Grads by Lionel
Trilling, D. Litt., a masterpiece, I thought,
of academic prose, so clear and yet
so dark. It cheers me that you do not change

at Harvard, like *castrati* whose voices
retain their boyish purity. Trilling
delights me with his cadenced double-talk.
"The radical," says he, and dares to add
"subversive" in a breathless tone, is like
to be predominant among the forces of
our time. Already on the student mind
(so impatient of the rational) this force
works powerfully. Oppose it, counsels he,
in order that it may grow strong and strike
deep roots. "Bland tolerance," he trills, "subverts"
subversion, makes it wither on the vine.
The way to nurse dissent is to impose
conformity—the logic's Lionel's—
and carefully exclude dissenters from
the faculty. Would we aid William Blake
to mew his mighty youth? Deny stipends.
Give ninnies suck at Alma Mater's teats.
Wean Blake. Choose Doodle in his stead as Poet
in Residence lest William be suborned
by excess of ease and lick the arses that
require booting. The University
of Hard Knocks is the proper berth for such
obstreperous geniuses. "When we are scourged,
they kiss the rod, resigning to the Will
of God," as Swift observed of moralists
like Trilling. Fend from me, I beg you, sir,
offers of chairs magnates endow. Waylay
me with no teaching sinecure. (Degrees
sufficient to impress the Dean are mine.)
Summon me never to recite my verse
before a convocation in my honor
nor to appear in doctoral costume
as orator at Commencement. Such coddling,
as Trilling rightly says, would work my ruin.
Let me forever cope with penury
and cold neglect. Let me be ostracized
for practicing ideals you fine folk
are given to prating of at ceremonies.
Do what you please with me defunct. Put up
a plaque. Dissect my corpse in seminars.
Transmogrify my bones to index cards.
Hang my dead portrait in the library
and crucify your living rebels still.

INDEXES

Index of First Lines

Index of Titles